AF552438

ENVIRONMENTAL WASTE MANAGEMENT

ENVIRONMENTAL WASTE MANAGEMENT

A Study of Cellulosic Wastes from Slaughter Houses

By
Dr. (Mrs.) J.P. Shastri

ANMOL PUBLICATIONS PVT. LTD.
NEW DELHI - 110 002 (INDIA)

ANMOL PUBLICATIONS PVT. LTD.
4374/4B, Ansari Road, Daryaganj
New Delhi - 110 002
Ph.: 23261597, 23278000
Visit us at: www.anmolpublications.com

Environmental Waste Management

First Published, 2004

ISBN 81-261-1485-1

PRINTED IN INDIA

Published by J.L. Kumar for Anmol Publications Pvt. Ltd., New Delhi - 110 002 and Printed at Mehra Offset Press, Delhi.

Contents

Preface

Though India is predominantly an agricultural economy, paradoxically it has a perpetual shortage of animal feeds. Against the backdrop of unplanned expansion in animal farming and prevalent calorie as well as protein malnutrition in more than 60% of the animals, there is an imperative need for expanding our food horizon.

Concurrent with the expansion of livestock breeding, there is an alarming increase in the wastes of slaughter houses and meat processing plants. Around 214 million bovines are slaughtered annually in about 3,600 authorized slaughter houses in India. On the whole about 4.6 million tonnes of ruminal waste is thus produced.

The rumen ingesta which is essentially a lignocellulosic waste with high BOD and COD values, creates a gigantic problem of disposal. The methods generally adopted are uneconomical as well as environmentally unsafe.

The large quantities of rumen ingesta regularly available at the slaughter houses have a great potential as substitute for protein upgradation and animal feed.

In this book, an explorative effort has been made to ferment the substrate to mycoproteins using a fungus *Pencillium simplicissimum.* Submerged as well as solid state fermentations have been studied alongwith the various parameters affecting their kinetics. Nutritional evaluation studies of the same in poultry were encouraging.

The bio-conversion of rumen ingesta is suggested as an ecologically safe and economically viable alternative method. It will not only be a solution for waste disposal but also for protein malnutrition in our animals.

This book would be useful for students of applied microbiology, biotechnology, agriculture and veterinary sciences as well as personnel involved in waste disposal at slaughter houses and meat processing plants.

I place on record my deep sense of gratidude to Dr. Yvonne Freitas, University of Mumbai and Dr. V.L. Paranjape, Mumbai Veterinary College, Konkan Krishi Vidyapeeth, Mumbai.

—Dr. (Mrs.) Jayagouri P. Shastri

1

Introduction

With 368.4 million animals and 486.7 million tonnes of feeds available, India has the unique distinction of having the largest livestock population in the world with perhaps the lowest per capita availability of animal feeds. Though our country is endowed with vast resources for agricultural and industrial development, our animals constantly face the problem of hunger and malnutrition. Recurring drought conditions, conversion of grazing lands into croplands, industrial development, diversion of straw to cellulose-based industries and unplanned expansion in animal farming have all led to a deteriorating supply of conventional fodder.

The estimated availability of the conventional fodder and feeds i.e. green fodder, crop residues and feed concentrates for the bovine population in India is about 30% of the requirement (Report C.F.G., 1987). From the projected livestock population and feed availability in the next decade (Report N.C.A. 1980) it is evident that the food stocks are too meagre to sustain the animals in a healthy state.

Against this background of dwindling feed resources and the prevalent calorie as well as protein malnutrition in about 60% of the animals (Soni, 1979) there is an imperative need for expanding our food horizons without disturbing the ecological balance. Preservation, ensiling and efficient recycling of agricultural and agro-based industrial wastes and exploitation of unconventional sources of proteins are some of the important approaches.

One of the most attractive methods of producing protein is through the rapid growth of micro-organisms on wastes. These can be cultivated, not only on a variety of waste substrates, but also a thousand times faster than plants and animals (Sandhya et al., 1984).

The concept of using microorganisms for human consumption is not a recent innovation and their use as flavour enhancers in cheese, *miso* and tempeh is well established (Hesseltine, 1965). During World War II, fungi grown on whey and the spent mass of **Penicillium chrysogenum** from penicillin fermentation were utilized as feed supplements for poultry (Fink et al., 1930).

In 1966, a new term 'Single Cell Protein' (SCP) was coined at the Massachusetts Institute of Technology, U.S. by Prof. C.L. Wilson to replace the older term 'Microbial proteins' (Scrimshaw, 1968).

In the seventies many processes of cell mass cultivation were developed with a variety of substrates e.g. the algae **Scenedesmus** spp. and **Spirullina** on CO_2 and sunlight (Durand Chastel & Clement, 1975); **Methylococcus** on methane (Harwood & Pirt, 1972); **Candida** spp. on a n-alkanes and sulphite waste liquor (Ridgeway et al., 1975); **Penicillium cyclopium** on whey (Kim & Lebeault, 1981) and **Scytalidium acidophilum** on waster paper (Ivarson & Morita, 1982).

The filamentous fungi were preferred for protein production because of numerous favourable characteristics such as their ability to degrade a wide range of complex substrates with simple nutritional requirement, their tolerance and preference for low pH which prevents infection and contamination, their ability to penetrate insoluble materials which permits their cultivation on solid substrates, their easily recoverable biomass, their fibrous structure and faint mushroom like odour which makes them more readily acceptable, their high protein in the range 35-50% and a lower nucleic acid content than yeast and bacteria and their digestibility and net protein utilization, which are much higher than most SCP organisms (Chahal, 1982).

However the choice of fungi as a protein organism, has been criticized for their negative characteristics such as poorer growth rates, slightly lower nutritional values than yeast and bacteria, difficulty in aerating their rheologically complex fermentation broths and for undersirable metabolites like oxalic acid and mycotoxins (Solomons, 1985).

In practice, due to and despite the above characteristics, many species of fungi have been used in biomass cultivation processes. **Paecilomyces variotii** cultivated on striped sulphite waster liquor (Romantschuk, 1975; Romantschuk & Lehtomaki, 1978), **Chaetomium cellulolyticum** grown on corn stover (Moo Young et al., 1979b) and **Geotrichum candidium** on whiskey distillery wash (Quinn & Merchant, 1979) are a few of the fungi cultivated and approved for animal feeds.

The culmination of all research on fungal proteins was the approval of the "Mycoprotein" produced by Rank **Hovis MacDougal**, U.K., with the fungus **Fusarium graminearum** ATCC 20334, for human consumption after a series of safety evaluation programmes (Gellender, 1981).

The revival of interest in Mycoproteins can be attributed to the fact that after the prohibitive rise in prices of hydrocarbons, cellulosic wastes have been accepted as the world's largest and most renewable sources of carbon and energy which can be economically used as substrates for fermentation by fungi (Meteles, 1979).

Lignocelluloses which are mainly composed of cellulose, hemicellulose and lignin (Mark, 1954) possess high degree of polymerization and crystallinity and are recalcitrant to chemical and enzymatic hydrolysis (Rose, 1979). Hence any microbial process aimed at conversion of lignocelluslose to proteins includes a pretreatment step in order to render the cellulose more accessible (Cowling, 1975).

A number of physical, chemical and enzymatic treatments have been tried before cultivation of fungi (Fan et al., 1982) Bungay, 1983). Milling by different methods is extensively used for decreasing the crystallinity index (Ghose & Kostic 1969; Pardes-Lopez & Gonsalez, 1973; Tassinari et al., 1982). Steam treatment (Detroy et al., 1979). pyrolysis (Buchholz et al., 1981) and irradiation by Gamma rays (Kamukura & Kaetsu, 1983) have been reported to have a depolymerizing and oxidative effect on cellulose.

A wide variety of chemicals like acids (Gansalez & Moo Young, 1981), NaOH (Chahal et al., 1978), oxidising agents (Gould, 1985), ammonia (Han & Callihan, 1974) and solvents like butanol and ethylene diamine (Taniguchi, et al., 1982) have been used for delignification.

For improving the accessibility of cellulosic substrates without chemical agents, selective lignin degradation has been proposed by using some organisms or their filtrates e.g. brown rot fungi (Konigs, 1972), enzymes of the white rot fungus **Sporotrichum pulverulentum** (Eriksson, 1974), white rot fungi (Zadrazil, 1983) and a mycelial fungus **Chetomium piluferum** (Kirk & Farrel, 1987). Recently, the use of the saprophytic actinomycete **Streptomyces viridosporus** (Ramchandra et al., 1987) and some rumen microorganisms (Akin & Benner, 1988) have been studied, for delignification of agro-wastes.

Fermentation of Lignocelluloses to Mycoproteins

Native cellulose has been converted to useful proteins by various methods: (1) Chemical hydrolysis of cellulose and growth of microorganisms on the hydrolysate (2) Enzymatic hydrolysis of cellulose to glucose and fermentation of sugar by microorganisms (3) Hydrolysis by one intact organism and conversion of hydrolysis products of protein by another organism (4) Hydrolysis of cellulose and protein production by a single organism (Callihan & Clemmer, 1979).

Chemical Hydrolysis of Cellulose Followed by Microbial Growth

Commercial hydrolysis of lignocelluloses has been categorised under two general approaches, that of high acid concentration at low temperature (Grethlein, 1978) or low acid concentration at high temperature, (Oshima, 1965). 1 to 5% H_2SO_4 at 121°C hydrolyses mainly the hemicellulose component. Higher temperature and prolonged heating however, further degrade the sugars to furfural which is toxic to microbial growth and animals (Chahal et al., 1977).

H_2SO_4 has been used for saccharification of various substrates like cellulose powder (Roberts et al., 1980), paper mill sludge (Paquot & Herman, 1983), wheat straw and aspen wood (Grohmann et al., 1985).

Candida utilis has been cultivated on acid hydrolysates of waste cotton (El-Nawawy, 1969), kenaf stems (Nagy et al., 1975) and rice straw (Tuse et al., 1981). Fungi like **Fusarium spp.** (Christias et al., 1975) and **Aureobasidium**

pullulans (Han et al., 1976a) have been used to ferment grass straw and hydrolysates.

Enzymatic Saccharification of Cellulose and Growth of Microrganisms on The Sugar

Cellulases are complex microbial enzymes which hydrolyse celluloses and are made up of a number of synergistic components (Mandels & Reese, 1964). These have been further classified as

(1) Endo-β (1-4) glucanases
(2) Exo-β (1-4) glucanases
  (i) Cellobiohydrolase
  (ii) Glucohydrolase
(3) β-glucosidase (Petterson et al., 1972).

Cellulases being induced enzymes, are produced only when the organism is grown in presence of cellulose, cellobiose, lactose, sophorose and other glucans with β (1 -4) linkages (Gritzaali & Brown, 1979). The mode of attack of these enzymes has been discussed by Ghose and Ghosh (1978) and Chang et al., (1981).

Extensive literature on the biochemistry and kinetics of cellulase is available e.g. cellulase biosynthesis and regulation (gong & Tsao, 1979), cellulase Kinetics (Nisizawa, 1973), properties and purification (Emert, 1974; Wood, 1975), hyperproduction by mutants (Bisaria & Ghose, 1981; Joglekar et al.,1983; Araujo, 1984) and applications of cellulases on various forms of celluloses (Hajny & Reese, 1969).

Genetic engineering (Gilkes et al., 1984, Sacco et al., 1984) and cloning of cellulase genes into **E. coli** (Whittle et al., 1982; Toyoma et al., 1984) for improvement of yields have met with limited success.

Enhancement of cellulase activity by control of the fermentation process has been extensively studied e.g. fed batch cultures Hendy et al (1982; 1984), continuous cultures (Mitra & Wilke, 1975; Alien & Mortenson, 1981), cell holding continuous cultures (Taniguchi et al., 1982) and continuous cultures with cell recycling (Ghose & Sahai, 1979).

Process improvements for better yields have been devised by Bastawde et al. (1978). Opoku and Adoga (1980); Chidambareswaran et al., 1986 and Ladisch et al., (1983). Technical and economic constraints of various processes based on different cellulosic substrates have been discussed in the proceedings of a number of symposia (Reese, 1962; Bailey et al.,1975; Yamanke & Wilke, 1976; Ghose, 1978; Neijssel et al., 1987).

Among the cellulolytic microorganisms the most thoroughly studied organism, for its enzymatic saccharification is **Trichoderma viride** (Tanaka & Matsuno,1985). Its enzyme activity has been studied by batch cultivation (Andreotti et al., 1978; Gallo et al., 1978; Mukhopadhyay, 1980), continuous cultivation (Brown et al., 1975; Jagannathan et al.,1975; Mandels et al.,1975; Sahai and Ghose 1978; Ryu et al.,1979) and by immobilisation on various polymers (Spasov et al.,1987).

A number of other species including **Trichoderma harzinum.** (Saddler et al., 1983), **Trichoderma longibrachiatum** in a mixed culture with **Scytalidium lignicola** (Trivedi & Ray,1985) have been studied for enzymatic hydrolysis.

The other genera of molds utilized for saccharification of agricultural and forestry residues are **Aspergillus fumigatus** NRC 272 (Shaker et al., 1984); **Aspergillus nidulans** (Bagga, Sandhu, 1987); **Aspergillus niger** (Giles et al.,1987) and **Aspergillus japonicus** (Sanyal et al., 1988).

The genus **Penicillium** has been widely studied for its cellulase e.g. **Penicillium citrinum** (Dave, 1983); **P. funiculosum** (Khandeparker, 1976; Joglekar et al., 1983; Rao et al., 1984; Seeta 1987) **P. pinophilum and P. purpurogenum** (Take et al., 1985).

Many other cellulolytic fungi like **Humicula** sp. (Sounder & Chandra, 1988), **Pellicularia spp.** (Kamikubo, et al., 1981), **Pestalotiopsis versicolor** (Thakur et al., 1982), **Thermoascus aurantiacus** (Feldman et al., 1988). **Thilvavia sepedonium** (Bagool, 1982), **Verticillium** sp. and other marine fungi (Araujo, 1978) have been investigated for saccharification of agricultural wastes. The saccharified product has been generally fermented to SCP by **Candida utilis, Saccharomyces cereviseae** (D'Souza, 1972) or sometimes by yeasts like **Candida marina and Rhodotorula** marina (Araujo & D'Souza, 1980). A simultaneous enzymatic saccharification and fermentation of cellulose with a yeast **Brettanomyces clauserii** in Solid Substrate Fermentation has been reported by Wyman et al., (1986).

Cellulose Hydrolysis and Fermentation by Two Different Intact Organisms

In order to eliminate the need for separate production of cellulose enzymes and the saccharification step, the substrate can be directly fermented by a selected mixed culture. The combination of two or more organisms is such that the first organism is celulolytic, while the second one can utilize the hemicellulose monomers and glucose to grow rapidly and increase the cell mass. The combinations of this type often exhibit symbiosis (Bungay, 1983).

Han et al. (1971) and Rao (1978) investigated a mixture of two different cellulolytic organisms **Cellulomonas** sp. and **Alcaligenes** sp. for production of proteins from alkali pretreated rice straw and bagasse respectively.

Peiterson (1975b) examined a combination **of Trichoderma viride** QM 9414 and **Saccharomyces cereviseae or Candida utilis** on alkali treated barely straw; while Kristensen (1978) and Molina et al. (1984) combined **Cellulomonas** with **Candida utilis** on the same substrate. Chang et al. (1980) obtained protein from rice hulls with a co-culture of **Bacillus, Cellulomonas** and **Pseudomonas.**

A novel combination of a lignolytic white rot fungus **Sporotrichum pulverulentum** and a cellulolytic mycelial fungus **Chaetomium** sp. was tried on wheat straw (Prendergast et al.,1983). Similarly **Pleurotus** alongwith **Chatomium cellolyticum** was grown by solid subtrate fermentation. (Chahal, 1984).

Anaerobic bacteria, **Bacteriodes cellulosolvens** and **Clostridium saccharolyticum** (Murray, 1986) and yeast **Brettanomyces clauseri** and **Pichia stipitis** (Wayman et al., 1987) were grown in a co-culture for ethanol and SCP production from cellulosic wastes. A mixed culture of **Paecilomyces variotii** and **Candida utilis** yielded a rich biomass on the prehydrolysate liquor of a rayon pulp mill (Bajpai & Bajpai, 1988).

All the above combinations not only increased efficiency of fermentation but also speed up the process probably because of repression of end product inhibition of cellulases.

Hydrolysis and Biomass Production by a Single Organism

For this type of fermentation an organism that can produce a large amount of cellulase and give a protein rich biomass also, is generally used. It should be a non-toxic, food-grade organism, which can be cultivated and separated easily from the fermentation medium.

Conversion of cellulosic wastes to proteins by growth

of the organism directly on the substrate in generally an aerobic process which may be carried out by either submerged liquid fermentation or by solid substrate fermentation (SSF) (Knapp & Howell, 1980).

A number of fungi have been cultivated by the submerged process, for fermentation of different kinds of cellulosic wastes. **Aspergilus oryzae** was cultivated on agro-wastes by Cabrera et al., (1974). Other species of **Aspergillus** like **A. flavus** (Ali & Zaqidi, 1984). **A. niger** (Sethi & Grainger, 1981; Balden-Sperger et al., 1985)(and **A. terreus** (Singh & Kalra, 1978; Garg & Neelkantan, 1981, 1982a, b) were cultivated on rotten fruits and vegetables, banana wastes and corncobs respectively.

Chaetomium spp. have been most frequently cultivated for recycling of agro-wastes into animal feeds (Chachal, 1985). A variety of substrates such as wheat straw, rice straw and hulls (Araujo, 1978); paper pulp (Moo Young et al., 1977, 1978); acid and alkali treated sawdust, (Pamment et al., 1978), and piggery wastes (Chahal & Ishaque, 1984) have been fermented with **Chaetomium cellulolyticum,** a thermotolerant cellulolytic fungus. **Chaetomium globosum** was utilised for mycoprotein production from pretreated cornstalks (Chahal et al., 1978), solka floc (Miller & Srinivasan, 19790 and rice straw (Dhillon et al., 1980).

Myrothecium verrucaria was found to actively utilize ball milled newspaper (Updegraff, 1971) and wheat straw fraction (Singh & Kalra, 1978). **Paecilomyces variotii** was found to produce a rich biomass on prehydrolysate liquor of a rayon mill (Bajpai & Bajpai, 1988).

The genus **Penicillium** has been fairly popular for cultivation on agrowastes e.g. **P. chrysogenum, P. crustosum, P. funiculosum** and **P. janthinellum** (Chahal

& Cheema 1971; Stern & Gasner, 1974; Srinivasan et al., 1983).

Trichoderma viride and its mutants have been infrequently used for direct fermentation of cellulosic wastes like feed lot (Griffin et al., 1975) and ball-milled newspaper (Nystrom & Diluca, 1978). While the mutant **T. viride** QM 6A gave a good yield of protein on NaOH treated barley straw, **T. viride** QM 9123 was reported to give a poor protein recovery on newspaper (Peitersen, 1977).

Sporotrichum pulverulentum which degrades lignin and hemicelulose in preference to cellulose has been utilised for degradation of wastes like fibreboard mill effluent and waste fibres (Ek & Eriksson, 1975, 1978; Thomke et al., 1980); rice hulls (Janus, 1978), crop residues (Atal et al., 1978), and cassava (Smith et al., 1986).

Many other fungi like **Rhisoctonia solani** (Chahal & Gray, 1971), **Verticillium aboatrum** (Gupta & Heale 1971), **Fusarium moniliforme** (Macris & Kokke, 1978) and **Gliocladium** spp. (Klappach et al., 1984) have been grown on different agricultural residues.

Since submerged cultivations require rigorous control of pH, temperature, foaming, aeration and agitation and also, harvesting of the product becomes an uneconomical process due to the small particle size and low concentration of the substrate, solid substrate fermentation (SSF) of wastes have been recommended (Han, 1978).

SSF is especially useful when the supporting substrate need not be separated from the fungal mycelial mass as in animal feeds (Bailey & Ollis, 1977). This method which reduces fermentor volumes and permits high substrate to inoculum ratio with minimum process controls, has been studied for fermentation of a wide variety of cellulosic and non-cellulosic substrates (Aidoo et al., 1982).

Agricultural residues have been fermented by SSF in either silos, simple pans or in highly mechanised rotating drum fermentors (Mukhopadhyay & Pathak, 1973). Fungi similar to those used for submerged fermentation have been cultivated on solid substrate wheat straw e.g. **Trichoderma lignorum** (Viesturs et al., 1981) **Chaetomium cellulolyticum,** (Rosen & Schuegerl, 1983), **Sporotrichum pulverulentum and Candida utilis** (Ulmer, 1983) and **Strophoria rugosoannulata,** a white rot fungus (Kamra & Zadrazil, 1985).

SSF of other wastes like plant and leafy materials of alfalfa by **Aspergillus niger** and **Rhizopus nigricans** (Bajracharya & Mudget, 1979), city was wastes from market places by **Myceliophthora thermophila** (Sen et al, 1981), bagasse by **C. cellulolyticum** (Carrizales & Saenz, 1984), cassava by **Sporotrichum pulverulentum** (Smith, et al., 1986) and beet pulp by **Penicillium capsulatum** (Considine al., 1987) have yielded nutritionally upgraded fodder.

Fermentation of Animal Wastes

Animal wastes are rich in nutrients and can support the growth of a number of organisms. Though underutilized, some of them have been recycled as feed ingredients for livestock (Bhattacharya & Taylor, 1975; Kalra, 1980).

Feedlot wastes have been reused for cattle feeding after different types of submerged fermentation e.g. **T. viride** cellulase treatment, followed by autofermentation (Griffin et al., 1975), enrichment with **Thermoactionmyces** spp. (Humphrey et al., 1977) or anaerobic fermentation (Reddy & Erdman 1977). Feed lot wastes have also been upgraded by SSF methods with different organisms like the indigenous flora present (Hrubant, 1975), **Chaetomium cellulolyticum** (Ulmer et al., 1981) and **Pestalotiopsis versicolor** (Rao et al., 1983).

Piggery wastes which have a high nitrogenous content (McGill et al., 1978) were protein enriched by cultivation of organisms like **Anthrospira plantensis** (Chang et al., 1978) **Aspergillus niger** (Reddington & Brown, 1978; Winkler, 1983), the normal anaerobic flora (Ringpfeil et al., 1980) and **C. cellulolyticum** (Moo Young et al., 1981).

Cowdung was enriched in crude protein by mixing it with barley straw and fermenting it with **C. cellulolyticum** (Moo Young et al., 1979a) or by cultivation of the photosynthetic bacterium, **Rhodopseudomonas capsulatum** (Vrati & Verna, 1983).

Hence, lignocellulosics in the form of wastes from agriculture, forestry or animal breeding have been utilised for production of proteins or protein enriched fodder, by different microbiologial treatments. These proteins are usually nutritionally comparable to the reference protein of FAO/WHO (1965) except for a deficiency of methionine content (Solomons, 1985) and have been successfully used for substituting the conventional protein supplements in animal feeds (Moo Young et al., 1978). Though it is too early to recognise the economic and other long term benefits reaped by animal breeders through the large scale use of microbial enriched feeds, the success of many feeding trials in experimental animals prompts the exploration of newer sources of cellulosic wastes for microbial fermentation.

Till recently the rural practice of utilization of animal wastes for fuel and fertilizer purposes, solved the problem of disposal to a great extent. However, with urbanisation, expansion and development of livestock breeding and reorganisation of farms and slaughter houses in the vicinity of towns, there is an alarming increase in the by-products and wastes of slaughter houses and meat processing plants. Residues like bones, hides, horns, hooves, blood, condemned offal, fat and gelatin are reutilized by different ancillary industries. However, huge amounts of rumen contents of slaughtered animals remain unclaimed and unutilized (Jobling, 1986).

There are about 2800-3000 authorised slaughter houses in India (Mandokhot, 1987; Muralidharrao, 1987), where about 214 million bovines are slaughtered per annum (FAO year book, 1999). Though data on the exact output of the rumen contents in India is not available (Muralidharao, 1987), on the whole, 1.84 million tonnes of waste is produced from animals (Ichhaponani and Lodhi, 1976).

Deonar abattoir situated in the suburbs of Bombay is the largest in S.E. Asia. In the year 2000-2001, 2.4 million head of cattle and 15 million sheep and goats were slaughtered. (Report, 2001). As a result, a daily average of 30-35 metric tonnes of rumen contents (rumen ingesta) are collected.

The rumen, which is the first compartment of the stomach of a ruminant, has a capacity of about 80-100 litres in large animals (Stanier et al., 1983). It serves as an incubation chamber for the ingested feed stuffs, which are mixed with copious amounts of saliva and rumen flora. Cattle fodder being highly fibrous, the rumen ingesta is characterized by a relatively low crude protein and high crude fibre and energy content (Reddy, 1986). The composition of rumen ingesta, like all animal wastes, is subject to variation, but it is essentially made up of cellulose, hemicellulose, lignin, starch, and minerals. The pH is in the range 5-7 (near neutrality). Since it can support the growth of a number of organisms, its BOD and COD is relatively high.

The rumen ingesta if allowed to ferment uncontrolled, putrifies and creates a massive problem of disposal. Hence it is usually used as landfill, incinerated or released into water courses. Such an approach is not only uneconomical but environmentally unsafe leading to depletion of dissolved oxygen, loss of aquatic life and recyclable plant cellulose.

Hence the present study was undertaken with the aim of determining whether this slaughterhouse waste, with a negative value could be used as a substrate for cultivating microorganisms and recycled into high protein fodder.

This could help solve two long standing needs, one of a pollution abatement process and the other of a low cost unconventional protein.

2

Pretreatment and Chemical Analysis of Rumen Ingesta

In order to understand the degradation of rumen ingesta or any other lignocellulose some knowledge about its chemical nature is essential.

Cellulose is a linear polymer of anhydro glucose units linked at the 1 and 4C atoms by a Beta-glucoside bond (Mark, 1954). In all plant materials cellulose is associated with hemicellulose, lignin, silica, pectin and some other substances. Hemicellulose is a complex polymer made up of many sugars. Lignin, a hetrocyclic polymer and a non-carbohydrate fraction not only acts as a binder to maintain physical strength, but also as a protective shield against microbial attack. Consequently the native cellulose fibres are resistant to chemical and enzymatic degradation and as such are poor fermentation substrates (Ghose 1978).

Rapid and complete penetration by chemicals or enzymes can be achieved by pretreatment of the substrate by physical, chemical or enzymatic methods. Treatments like milling, steaming under pressure, Gamma irradiation and chemical treatment with swelling agents like acids and alkalis are some of the widely favoured methods.

Materials and Methods

Pretreatment: Rumen ingesta samples were mixed and

oven dried at 80° C to a constant weight. The samples were then subjected to various physical and chemical pretreatments as follows:

1. 100 g sample was hammermilled to 1 -2 mm particle size and weighed.
2. 100 g hammermilled rumen ingesta was taken in an Erlenmeyer flask and autoclaved at 121.6 C for 30 min. and 15 psig.
3. 100 g each of hammermilled sample were placed in four polythene bags. To two of these bags, 10 ml of distilled water was added to moisten the sample. All the four bags were sealed and placed in a ^{60}Co Gamma cell and irradiated. One bag each of dry and moist sample was irradiated with a total dosage of 10^8 rads and the other two bags to a dosage of 5 x 10^8 rads.
4. 100 g of hammermilled sample was mixed with one litre each of 1 to 5% NaOH solutions in separate flasks, in duplicate sets. One set was incubated RT for 2h. Another set was autoclaved at 121° C and 15 psig for 30 min. All the treated samples were washed repeatedly to neutrality and ovendried at 80° C to a constant weight.
5. An untreated sample of rumen ingesta was taken as control.

Evaluation of Pretreatment

1. Yield from pretreatment was calculated by deducting the weight of the dried substrate after the pretreatment from that of the original weight of sample.
2. Percentage of delignification. The lignin content was determined by the method of Goering and Van Soest, (AOAC, 1970). The difference between

the lignin content of the untreated and treated samples was determined.

3. Evaluation of Digestibility: The effect of various treatment variables on the digestibility of the substrate was determined by the standard substrate test procedure (Rockwell, 1976):
   i. 1 g of untreated and treated samples of rumen ingesta were added to 100 ml of **Trichoderma viride** basal medium (Mandels and Weber, 1969)) in 250 ml Erlenmeyer flasks.
   ii. The flasks were autoclaved and then inoculated with 10 ml of a mycelial pellet culture of the M-21 fungus which was isolated in the studies.
   iii. All flasks were incubated on a rotary shaker (200 rpm) for 6 days to 28-33 C.
   iv. The contents of the flasks were harvested by filtration through tared whatman No. 1 filterpaper, washed and dried at 80 C for 24 h. The percentages of dry matter yield and protein recovery were determined.
4. Chemical Composition: The untreated, coarsely chopped (A) and 5% NaOH treated (with autoclaving) (B) samples were subjected to proximate analysis of their chemical composition.

The ether extract content was determined using petroleum ether with Boiling Point 40-60 C (AOAC, 1970).

The crude protein was calculated by the Kjeldahl method (Standard Methods, 1975).

The crude fiber, lignin, cellulose, hemicellulose contents were determined by the method of Goering and Van Soest (AOAC, 1970).

Results

Effects of Pretreatment (Table 2.1)

Dry matter yield : All the physical methods of the pretreatment gave a higher dry matter yield than alkali treatment. With gamma irradiation, there was almost no dry matter loss.

TABLE 2.1

Effect of Pretreatment

Type of Pretreatment	*Lignin content* %	*Deligni-fication* %	*Yield from Pre-treatment* %	*Protein recovery g/100 g substrate*
Untreated	12.2	-	100	2.4
Hammermilled	12.2	-	94.2	4.8
Autoclaved	12.1	0.97	92.6	4.9
Gamma 10^8 rads (dry)	-	-	94.2	5.2
-"- 5 x 10^8 rads(dry)	-	-	-"-	13.5
-"- 10^8 rads (wet)	-	-	-"-	6.3
"5 x 10^8 " rads (wet)	-	-	-"-	149
1%NaOH RT	12.0	1.6	90.4	62
2% -"-	11.6	3.2	88.5	6.5
3% -"-	11.0	10.6	82.6	7.2
4% -"-	10.6	13.1	78.5	9.1
5% -"-	10.4	14.8	74.8	9.5
1%NaOH AC	9.8	19.6	71.9	12.1
2% -"-	9.2	24.6	70.2	12.3
3% -"-	7.3	40.2	65.5	13.6
4% -"-	7.0	42.6	63.3	14.8
5% -"-	6.2	49.2	58.3	15.8

RT Room Temperature AC Autoclave

Delignification: The percentage of delignification was marginal in case of autoclaving. However, with alkali treatment, both at RT and at 121° C, the delignification was directly related to the concentration of NaOH used. With 5% NaOH treatment at RT, the delignification was 14.8%, which improved more than three times to 49.2% on autoclaving. Protein recovery per 100g substrate was calculated after appropriate deduction of inherent protein content before treatment.

Hammermilled and autoclaved samples gave a very low yield of protein, 4.8 and 4.9 g/100g substrate respectively. Gamma irradiated substrate yielded 6.3 and 14.9g protein per 100g substrate with 10^8 and 5 x 10^8 rads respectively on wet substrate which is significant, whereas the same doses on dry samples yielded 5.2 and 13.5g/100g protein respectively.

The overall protein recovery was the highest i.e 15.8g/ 100g with 5% NaOH treated, autoclaved sample. The same treatment at RT gave a protein recovery of 9.5g/100g substrate. The protein recovery was observed to be directly related to the extent of delignification.

Chemical composition: (Table 2.2) From the proximate analysis of the untreated (A) and 5% NaOH + autoclaved (B) samples of rumen ingesta, it was seen that the crude fibre content increased from 38.90% to 73.36% while the ether extract content decreased from 1.59% to 1.38% on treatment.

The crude protein content sample of A was 7.63% and of B was 1.57%. The ash content was around 10% in both cases, while the lignin content decreased from 13.09 in A to 7.22% in sample B. The cellulose content was 36.35 in A which proportionately increased to 51.95% in B. The hemicellulose content however decreased from 27.10% to 23.70%.

TABLE 2.2

Proximate Analysis of Rumen Ingesta

	A *Untreated*	*B* *5% NaOH (AC)*
Crude fibre	38.90	73.36
Crude fibre (% on DMB)		
Ether extract	1.59	1.38
Crude protein	7.63	1.57
Ash	9.98	10.34
Lignin	13.09	7.22
Cellulose	36.35	51.95
Hemicellulose	27.10	23.70
Others	4.26	3.84

DMB Dry Matter basis

Discussion

Hammermilling was found to be an insufficient method of pretreatment for the rumen ingesta fibres which were partly reduced in particle size due to chewing by the animals.

Stranks (1959) and Dehority and Johnson (1961) found that ball milling of forages enhanced digestion in rumen. Milling was later recorded as a useful method of pretreatment before fermentation by many authors (Updegraff 1971; Mandels et al., 1974, 1975; Andren et al., 1976; Janus, 1978; Singh and Kalra, 1978 and Tassinari et al., 1982).

In agreement with our results, some authors have found that milling by itself was an insufficient method, though it proved to be essential for proper delignification by chemical methods.

Steaming under pressure without addition for chemicals (Mac Donald and Mathews, 1979) was found to separate lignin, hemicellulose and cellulose, convert them into a susceptible form for further conversion and àlso render the inhibitors more extractable (Waymen et al., 1980; Sinitsyn et al., 1982). However, it was found in this investigation was inadequate as indicated by the poor protein recovery.

Gamma irradiation at 5 $\times$ 10^8 rads yielded not only very good dry matter but also a good protein yield. 14.9g of protein obtained per 100g of wet substrate is comparable to the yield obtained with 4% NaOH + heat treatment. However a dosage of 10^8 rads was found to be inadequate. The enhancement in the protein production with a dosage of 5 X 10^8 rads and a moist substrate corroborates the results of Kamakura and Kaetsu (1982; 1983; 1984).

Digestibility of forages was found to increase with milling (Pritchard et al., 1962) or acid and alkali treatment before irradiation (Han et al., 1980). The net effect of Gamma irradiation on pure cellulose is oxidative degradation, dehydration and destruction of anhydro-glucose units, to yield CO_2 and cellulose chain cleavage which generate pentoses and hexoses (Klein et al., 1970; Linko, 1977; Fan et al., 1981).

Though autoclaving and NaOH treatment at RT individually did not yield a good delignification or protein recovery, the same treatments when combined brought about an almost 50% delignification. A higher concentration of alkali or longer period of heat treatment was found unnecessary because delignification beyond 50% leads to a collapse in the lignocellulosic structure, causing shrinkage of available surface area and recrystallization of cellulose (Fan et al., 1981).

With 5% NaOH + autoclaving, the protein recovery increased from 2.4 to 15.8g/100g substrate. This can be explained by the fact that aqueous solution of alkali can cause intercrystalline and intracrystaline swelling and breaking the H bond of a cellulose molecule (Schurz, 1978). This leads to an increase in the internal surface area, decrease in the degree of polymerisation and crystallinity, separation of structural linkages between lignin and carbohydrates and disruption of the lignin structure (Fan et al., 1982). Hence it has been widely favoured for pretreatment of lignocellulose (Han & Callihan, 1974; Daugalis & Bone, 1978).

The results obtained are in agreement with those obtained by Jaganathan et al., (1975) who reported an increase from 3% to 16% in the protein yield after 1 M NaOH treatment. Trivedi and Ray (1985) obtained a maximum delignification and protein yield with 10% NaOH + heat treatment for 1h.

Patil (1985) found an eight fold improvement in the bioconversion efficiency for the solid substrate fermentation of straw after NaOH treatment. Seeta (1987) made a pertinent observation that the effectiveness of any method of pretreatment depends on the nature of the substrate, when it was found that ball milling was more effective for pure cellulose and chemical treatment was better in case of lignocelluloses.

Proximate analysis of the untreated and NaOH +heat treated samples showed that the heat labile protein content which was 7.63% in the untreated sample was reduced during alkali cooking. Similarly hemicellulose contents were reduced, because of the water soluble nature of some of the pentosans (Ghose, 1978). The delignification with

5% alkali + heat treatment is sufficient to enable the organism to utilize the substrate better, compared to the untreated samples. 36% and 52% of cellulose and 13% and 7% of lignin content in samples A and B respectively fall within the range reported for different types of agricultural residue (Slonekar, 1976; Trivedi and Ray, 1985; Rai and Mudgal, 1987).

Considering the results of the proximate analysis and substrate utilization tests, it can be concluded that rumen ingesta is a challenging but rich source of cellulose for fermentation by microorganisms.

3

Screening of Cellulolytic Microorganisms

Decomposition of cellulose in nature especially in soil, is primarily and mainly carried by molds, followed by unicellular bacteria and actinomycetes (Waksman and Skinner, 1926).

Hungate (1944), Siu (1951) and Imsenecki (1968) have listed a number of organisms which can grow on cellulosic materials. Many of them have been isolated and studied extensively (Betrabet et al., 1968;Bhattacharya, 1974; Kelkar, 1977). Cellulolytic mycoflora have been screened from soil (Ahmed, 1982; Bagool, 1982) as well as wastes of paper and pulp industries (Ghate, 1984; Dudhbhate, 1985).

The cellulolytic activity of microorganism has been evaluated by various methods which include measuring (i) loss in the weight of cellulosic substrate, gravimetrically or colorimetrically (Halliwell, 1957) (ii) alteration in the infrared and X-rays pattern (Cowling and Kirk 1975) (iii) loss in tensile strength (Blum and Stahl, 1952) (iv) fall in the viscosity of soluble cellulose derivatives (Walseth, 1952; Manning, 1981) (v) saccharifying activity (Somogyi & Nelson,1952) (vi) width of a zone of clearance around the colony on cellulose agar (Rautella and Cowling, 1966; Montenecourt and Eveleigh, 1977) (vii) yield of biomass produced and gain in its protein content (Peitersen, 1975 a,b; Rockwell, 1976).

Though fungi can grow in the filamentous, pelleted or single cell form, almost all work on biomass production has involved filamentous growth (Solomons, 1985). Siu (1951) found many of the cellulolytic fungi to be either pathogenic or mycotoxic. Wyllie and Morehouse (1978) have discussed various methods of identifying mycotoxin producers.

Materials and Methods

Sample collection: For isolation of cellulolytic organisms, different samples were collected viz. (i) rumen ingesta (ii) rumen liquor from Deonar abattoir, Bombay (iii) elephant dung from Jeejamata Udyan, Byculla, Bombay (iv) decaying hay (v) soil samples from byres, Bombay Veterinary College, Bombay.

Enrichment Culture Technique: 100 ml of the four media (Table 3.1) were taken in 250 ml flasks and sterilized. 0.5g or 0.5ml of the sample was inoculated into all the four different media. The flasks were incubated on a rotary shaker at room temperature (RT) till the filter paper/ rumen ingesta fibres/cellulose was shredded/ diminished. 1 ml of each of the culture was transferred to a similar medium and reincubated. The process was repeated once more.

Isolation: 0.1 ml of the enrichment culture was either directly or after appropriate serial dilution, inoculated on to the respective media solidified with 2% agar. The plates were incubated at RT till there was visible growth. With the help of a stereoscopic microscope, the colonies with either clearance around the colony or showing discoloration, sliminess or shredding of filter paper were Observed and purified.

TABLE 3.1

Enrichment Media for Cellulolytic Bacteria

Rockwell, (1976)	*g/L*	*Mcbeth's medium*	*g/L*
$(NH_4)SO_4$	6.0	K_2HPO_4	1
NaCl	6.0	$MgSO_4.7H_2O$	1
K_2HPO_4	4.45	$An.Na_2CO_3$	1
KH_2PO_4	3.40	$(NH_4)_2SO_4$	2
$MgSO_4.7H_2O$	0.4	Cellulose/filter paper	1
$CaCl_2$	0.1		
Yeast extract	0.1		
Trace mineral sol.	1.0		
Cellulose/Rumen ingesta	1.0		
Trace mineral sol.	mg/ 100 ml		
$FeCl_3.6H_2O$	16.76		
$ZnS0_4.7H_2O$	0.18		
$CuS0_4.7H_2O$	0.16		
$CoCl_3.6H_2O$	0.18		
EDTA	20.10		

Enrichment Media For Cellulolytic Fungi

Trichoderma viride medium	*g/l*	*Penicillium funiculosum medium A*	*g/l*
KH_2PO_4	2.0	$NH_4H_2PO_4$	4.5
$(NH_4)_2SO_4$	1.4	KH_2PO_4	4.0
Urea	0.3	$MgSO_4.7H_2O$	0.3
$MgSO_4.7H_2O$	0.3	$CaCl_2.2H_2O$	0.3
$CaCl_2.2H_2O$	0.3	Tryptone	0.1
Cellulose/ Rumen ingesta	10.0	Polyethylene glycol	1.0
* Trace metal sol. (ml)	1.0	Cellulose	1.0
Peptone	0.01	* Trace metal sol. (ml)	1.0
		Tween - 80	200 ppm
pH5.6			
* Trace metal solution			
$FeSO_4\ 7H_2O$	500 mg		
$MnSO_4.H_2O$	150mg		
$ZnCl_2$.	167mg		
$CaCl_2$	200 mg		
19%HCl	10ml		
Distilled Water	100 ml		

Purification and Maintenance: All the isolates were purified on Nutrient/Potato dextrose agar plates and subcultured on slants of McBeth's cellulose agar (bacteria) and Trichoderma viride medium with filter paper strips (fungi). 2 sets each of the isolates were preserved at 4 C and periodically subcultured.

Primary Screening of the Isolates: All the isolates obtained were inoculated into 10 ml of McBeth's/T. viride medium containing a filter paper strip ($1^{\times}6$ cm) in test tube (18x150 mm), and incubated on the rotary shaker (200 rpm). The time in days required for almost complete shredding of the filter paper was noted for each culture. Those which showed positive results within 96 hours were filtered through fritted glass filters and the filtrates preserved at 4 C.

Secondary Screening of Isolates: The filtrates containing the cellulase enzyme were assayed for their Filter paper enzyme activity (FPA) by the method of Somogyi and Nelson (1952). One unit of Fpase is defined as one micromole of glucose equivalent released per hour under the condition of assay. A 1 x 6 cm strip of Whatman filter paper No. 1 weighing 50 mg was placed in a tube. To this 0.5 ml of the filtrate, 1 ml of 0.2 M acetate buffer (pH 5.6) and 0.5 ml of distilled water were added. The tubes were incubated at 50 C in a shaker water bath for 60 min. The reducing sugars formed were measured as D- glucose by the method of Somogyi and Nelson (1952).

Protein Production: The isolates were further screened for their ability to utilize rumen ingesta and gave a good yield of biomass and protein

(i) **Inoculum** : 96 h old mycelial growth of fungal isolates on **T. viride** medium slants and 48 old bacterial isolates on Mcbeth's cellulose agar slants were washed free of nutrients and inoculated into 100 ml of Czapek's broth (Difco Manual, 1969) and incubated on a rotary shaker for 72 and 48h respectively.

(ii) **Fermentation:** 1g of treated rumen ingesta was added to 100 ml each of modified **T. viride** medium and modified McBeth's medium in 250 ml Erlenmeyer flasks before sterilization. 10 ml of the inoculum was added to the respective media, which were incubated on a rotary shaker for 72 h.

(iii) **Harvesting:** The fungal biomass along with the unutilized substrate was filtered through tared Whatman No. 1 filterpaper and washed free of the medium. The bacterial biomass was harvested by centrifugation at 5000 rpm for 15 min washed twice. All the biomass samples obtained were dried at 80° C overnight and weighed. The protein content was determined by the Kjeldahl method.

Preliminary Screening for Mycotoxin Producers

(i) **Preparation of extract:** The fungal isolates which showed a high potential for protein production were grown in 100 ml of Potato dextrose broth for 72h. The cultures were then steamed for 30 min and filtered through fritted glass filter. The filtrate was mixed with 100 ml of chloroform in a stoppered flask and shaken for 10 min. The chloroform layer was separated by means of a separating funnel. In case of pigmented cultures, this was followed by a clean-up procedure by the Ferricgel method to remove pigments. The chloroform extract thus obtained was evaporated completely and the residue collected in one ml ethylene glycol and preserved at 4 C (Sharma et al., 1983).

(ii) **Thin Layer Chromatography:** 10 microlitres of the residue was spotted with standard controls on TLC plates of Silica Gel G. The plates were developed first in diethyl ether and then in a solvent system with chloroform: acetone: 2 propanol (825: 150; 25 V/V). The plates were then observed under U. V light of wavelength 254 nm and the intensity of each spot was compared with that of the standard. Rf values of the spots were calculated (Sharma et al. 1983).

(iii) **Inoculation of Mice:** The ethylene glycol extract was inoculated in 0.1 ml amounts into the peritoneal cavity of Swiss albino mice, with an average weight of 20 g. These, along with control mice were observed for 8 days (Wyllie and Morehouse, 1978).

Identification of the Selected Isolate

The fungal isolate found to be most suitable for protein production was selected was for further studies.

It was plated on Czapek Dox agar and Potato dextrose agar and identified on the basis of morphology, colony characteristics and various criteria suggested in literature reviews (Smith, 1960).

The bacterial isolate was plated on Mcbeth's cellulose agar and Nutrient agar. The culture was identified upto genus level on the basis of Gram staining, morphology and physiological characteristics (Bergey's manual, 1974).

Results

Isolation and Primary Screening: A total of 90 cellulolytic isolates consisting of 55 bacterial and 35 fungal cultures were obtained by enrichment culture technique with different media (Table 3.2).

TABLE 3.2

Habitatwise Distribution of The Cellulolytic Isolates

Type of organism	*Rumen Ingesta*	*Rumen liquor*	*Elephant Dung*	*Decaying hay*	*Byre soil*	*Total Isolates*
Gram Positive rods	1	-	1	2	1	5
Gram variable rods	5	3	2	1	1	12
Gram negative curved rods	3	1	2	-	-	6
Gram negative short rods	10	7	3	4	2	6
Gram positive oval forms	3	1	1	1	-	6
Fungi	11	7	3	9	5	35
	33	19	12	17	9	90

Eleven isolates were found to form a pulpy mass of filter paper strip within 96h. The short listed isolates consisted of six bacteria and five fungi (Table 3.3).

TABLE 3.3

Primary Screening of Isolates

Habitat	*Organisms Degrading Filter paper in 96 h*	
	Bacteria	*Fungi*
Rumen ingesta	4	1
Rumen liquor	1	1
Elephant dung	1	-
Decaying hay	-	2
Soil from byres	-	1
Total	6	5

Secondary Screening of Cellulolytic Isolates: On screening, the bacterial isolates showed poorer FPA as compared to the fungi; The mold isolates M-5, M-21 and M-35 produced 1.1, 0.9 and 1.0 FP units/ml of D-glucose which were the three highest values obtained (Table 3.4, Fig. 3.1.)

TABLE 3.4

Secondary Sereening of The Celluloytic Isolates

Isolate		*Source*	*F P ase Units per ml*	*DM mg/g substrate*	*Crude protein %*	*Pretein recovery g/100 g substrate*
Bacterial	B-5	Decaying hay	0.4	576	14.6	8.4
-"-	B-14	Rumen liquor	0.5	601	14.2	8.5
-"-	B-39	Rumen ingesta	0.3	563	14.9	8.4
-"-	B-42	Soil from byre	0.5	582	12.5	7.3
-"-	B-53	Rumen ingesta	0.6	613	14.7	9.0
-"-	B-54	-"-	0.7	596	16.4	9.8
Fungal	M-5	-"-	1.1	695	23.4	16.3
-"-	M-8	-"-	0.8	710	19.5	13.8
-"-	M-20	Decaying hay	0.8	704	22.8	16.1
-"-	M-21	-"-	0.9	682	24.8	16.9
-"-	M-35	Soil from byre	1.0	680	24.4	16.6

Figure 3.1. Secondary Scrseening of The Celluloytic Isolates (Fungal)

Biomass Yield and Protein 'Recovery: The dry matter yield (DMY) of biomass was observed to be higher with mold isolates, the highest being 610 mg/g substrate with M-8. The crude protein content of the biomass was higher in M-21 and M-35 which produced 24.8% and 24.4% respectively. The crude protein content of all the bacterial biomasses was lower than that obtained from molds. Habitat-wise grading showed that the overall protein recoveries

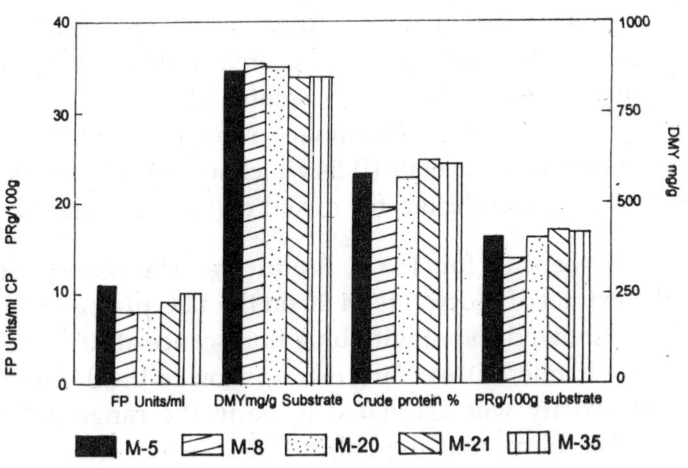

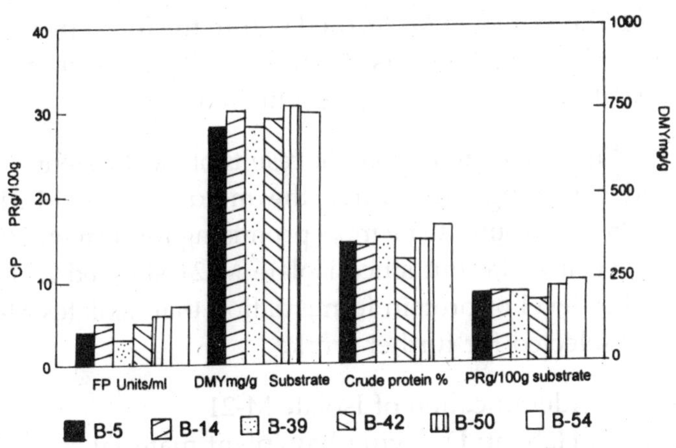

Figure 3.1. Secondary Screening of the Celluloytic Isolates (Fungal)

were maximum in isolates obtained from decaying hay as compared to those from other habitats.

It was also observed that there is no relation between the filter paper enzyme activity of an organism and its capability to produce a good protein yield when grown on rumen ingesta. The fungal isolates M-20, M-21 and M-35 were selected for preliminary screening for mycotoxin production. The isolate (B-54 which was the best of bacterial isolates) was selected for mixed culture fermentation.

Screening for Toxin Producers: The observation of the extract of the isolate M-20 on the TLC plates under U.V light showed a spot with blue florescence at Rf value 0.55. Since 10 microlitres of the extract showed the fluorescence, the toxicity was estimated to be in the range 0.02-0.055 ng/microlitre and the culture M-20 was excluded from further studies. The isolates M-21 and M-35, were retained as their extracts did not show any fluorescence.

On observation of the inoculated albino mice for 8 days, it was observed that a mouse which was injected with the extract of M-20, died within the first 24h, whereas the other two extracts did not elicit any symptoms of toxicity or illness in the experimental mice.

Final Selection: From the results of the different grading and screening procedures the mold isolates M-21 and M-35 were found to be most promising for fermentation of rumen ingesta, but since isolate M-21 showed a slightly higher level of protein fermentation than isolates M-35, it was selected for further work.

Identification of Isolate M-21
Habitat: Decaying hay/plant material.

Colony characteristics on Czapek-Dox and Potato dextrose agar: Pale blue green thick, velvety colonies with tough basal felt; slightly floccose or ropey but not funiculose. Exudate or transpiration fluid absent. Reverse of the colony, colorless to pale yellow.

Conidiophores: Size: 100 to 300 micrometers X 3.0 to 4.5 micrometers. Surface appears roughened.

Penicilli: Metulae few, 10 x 3 Micrometers each having two sterigmata, 6-8 x 2.5 micrometer. The metulae often gave the appearance of monoverticillate forms since sterigmata were not well defined. The sterigmata tapered towards the end from which conidia were formed.

Conidia: Elliptical to subglobose, generally 5 micrometer on long axis and 3 micrometers near the base, echinulate Some conidia were 8 x 4 micrometers.

Based on the criteria suggested in literature, habitat, cellulolytic activity and the morphology, the isolate was identified as **Penicillium simplicisimum** (Oudemans) Thorn. The identification was confirmed at the Naval Chemical and Metallurgical Laboratories, Bombay.

Identification of The Bacterial Isolate (Table 3.5). The isolate B-54 was identified on the basis of morphological, cultural and physiological characteristics, as a **Cellulomonas** sp. (Bergey's manual, 8th Ed., 1974).

Discussion

Of the different enrichment media used, McBeth's medium with a filter paper strip and **Trichoderma viride** medium (Mandels and Weber, 1969) with pure cellulose were found to yield the maximum number of cellulolytic bacteria and molds respectively.

TABLE 3.5

Taxonomic Features of the Bacterial Isolate B-54

Particulars	*Observations*
1. Morphological Characters	
Shape and Size	rods, 0.3 to 0.4 μm x 0.8 μm occurring singly, occasionally in beaded form.
Motility	non-motile
Gram stain	negative, weakly positive
Endospore formation	negative
2. Cultural characteristics	
Nutrient agar slants	ivory, glistening, raised and abundant
Nutrient broth	growth ivory, uniformly turbid
Cellulose agar plates	circular, 1.0 to 1.5 mm dia, colonies, smooth, glistening
Optimal temperature	28-33°C.
3. Physiological characteristics	
Fermentation of glucose, sucrose, cellobiose, xylose, maltose, lactose, mannose, galactose, arabinose	positive
Hydrolysis of starch and gelatin	positive
Vitamin and growth factors	not required
Catalase	positive
Decomposition of	positive
Carboxy methyl cellulose	
Methyl cellulose	poorly utilized
Filter paper	degraded
Ammonia production	positive
Nitrate assimilation	positive
Acid formation from carbohydrates	positive
Oxygen requirement	positive aerobic conditions favour growth on celulosic substrate.

Crude cultures of celluylolytic organism were obtained by Christiensen (1910) by inserting filter paper or linen cloth in soil. Nutrient salt medium with filter paper yielded relatively pure cultures (Omeliansky 1902; Dubos, 1928). Finely ground filter paper (Tetrault, 1930) and regenerated cellulose (Kellerman and McBeth, 1912; Walseth, 1952; Rautella and Cowling, 1966) yielded a better variety and number of cellulolytic organisms.

Improvement of mineral salt media (Mandels and Weber, 1969; Chahal and Gray, 1971; Reid, 1979; Garg and Neelkantan, 1981) yielded cellulolytic organisms with higher Fp activity.

Han and Srinivasan (1968) and Sarkar and Prabhu (1982) supplemented a mineral salt solution with 0.1% yeast extract. Peitersen (1975b) and Shaker et al. (1984) added 0.05% glucose and 0.01% peptone for initiating the growth of cellulolytic fungi. Addition of 0.01 mg/L of peptone to **Trichoderma viride** medium was found to be sufficient in the present studies for initiating growth of cellulolytic fungi and a concentration greater than 0.01 mg/L sometimes resulted in growth of non-cellulolytic forms.

An observation made with the stereoscopic microscope was that there was no relation between the growth of an organism on a cellulosic medium, the zone of clearance around the growth and its cellulolytic capability. This observation is supported by the findings of Mandels and Reese (1957) for **Trichoderma viride** and Moo Young et al. (1978) for **Chaetomium cellulolyticum** which grow poorly on CMC agar, but are established as highly cellulolytic organisms. These observations support our view that the cellulolytic activity of organisms cannot be judged from their growth characteristics on solid media.

However this is in contradiction to the report of Srinivasan and Han (1969) in which good growth of an organism on soluble CMS is considered as an indication of its ability to degrade cellulose.

Another relevant observation made from Table 3.4 was the lack of a direct relationship between the cellulolytic enzyme activity of an organism and the capability to produce good biomass with a high recovery of protein. Vogt and Staffeldt (1977) found a similar lack of a definite pattern between the biomass production of several fungi and the cellulolytic activity of their culture filtrates. Janus (1978) however, observed a lower cellulose activity in **Sporotrichum pulverulentum** cultures than **T. virdie** mutants but they showed a much better decomposition of cellulose and a higher protein yield than **T. viride.**

Griffin et al. (1975), Mandels et al. (1975) Chahal et al. (1977) and Garg and Neelkantan (1981) found an inverse relationship between good growth of fungi on cellulose media and cellulase enzyme activity.

Chahal et al. (1977) and Veisturs et al. (1981) found that enzyme activities in culture filtrates of non-treated straw were higher than those of treated straw. Lillehoj and Han (1983) observed a marked variation in the capacity of different fungi to produce extracellular enzyme and extracellar protein on various treated substrates. This phenomenon has been explained by assuming that since all or part of the cellulases are cell or substrate bound, they are not released into the culture filtrate when the organism stops growing. Viesturs et al., (1981) implicated the stronger absorption of the enzyme on treated substrates for its lower release into culture filtrate.

It was further observed that the dry matter yield and

the protein content of the biomass are inversely proportional. This may be explained by the assumption that the extra energy expended by an organism in producing a larger amount of crude protein results in a lesser yield of cell mass than in case of poorer crude protein producing organism. The substrate: mass balance for protein production of molds indicated that nearly half of the carbohydrate substrate is lost as carbon dioxide in the synthesis of high ordered biological macromolecules.

Hence, it can be safely concluded that comparison of cellulolytic activity of organisms grown on different substrates with different treatments cannot be made and secondly, while evaluating the potential of a SCP isolate, its capacity to produce a biomass with higher protein recovery is a far more important criterion than the FPA of its filtrates.

The mold isolate M-21 did not show any evidence of Mycotoxin production in the Chromatographic method nor did it show any undesirable reactions in the mice injected with its extract. Though the above methods of screening for toxin production by an isolate could be considered insufficient, they did serve the purpose of primary screening before further standardization of the fermentation process

The mold isolate M-21, showed a faster filterpaper degradation and a better yield of protein recovery from rumen ingesta than all the other isolates. It was tentatively adjudged to be free from toxin production, hence it was selected for further studies and identified as **Penicilium simplicissimum.** The genus **Penicillium** has an earlier history of being used for protein production on agricultural wastes e.g. **P. janthinellum** (Chahal and Cheema, 1971; Stern and Gasner, 1974; Srinivasan et al., 1983).

The bacterial isolate B-54 identified as **Cellulomonas** sp., showing best filter paper degradation and protein production amongst the bacterial isolates was selected for mixed culture fermentation.

4

Submerged Fermentation

Organisms, including fungi differ with respect to their preferences for environmental conditions, even species within the same genus reacting differently (Lilly and Barnet, 1951). Hence the optimum conditions of cultivation of an organism for its biomass or any other product have to be individually studied.

Fermentation parameters may be standardized in flasks (Singh and Kalra, 1978; Dhillon et al., 1982; Garg and Neelkantan, 1982 a, b; Sarkar and Prabhu, 1982), or laboratory fermentors by batch, fed batch cultivations (Brown and Halsted, 1975; Peitersen, 1975 B; Janus, 1978, Srinivasan et al., 1983), semicontinuous and continuous methods (Peitersen, 1975C; Miller and Srinivasan, 1983, Shaker et al., 1984).

Materials and Methods

Microorganism: The cellulolytic mold **Penicillium simlicissimum** isolated from decaying plant materials was used for all further studies. It was maintained on **T. viride** medium with filter paper strips as sole source of Carbon.

Inoculum: The fungus was cultivated in 100 ml Czapek's medium in shake flasks for 48h. The pelleted form of growth was centrifuged, washed and suspended in distilled water as to contain approximately 0.5 g/ml dry weight of mycelium. The isolate grown of Czapek's agar slants for 8 days was used for preparing a spore suspension with 10^7 spores/ml (counted in Petroff-Hausser chamber).

Fermentation Medium: The ingesta which was hammermilled, treated with 5% NaOH and autoclaved at 121C for 30 min (henceforth referred to as substrate) was used as sole cellulosic carbon source, at a 1% w/v level in **T. virdie** medium (Mandels and Weber, 1969). 100 ml of the medium was taken in 250 ml Erlenmeyer flasks, its pH adjusted to 5 and autoclaved; 1.5 litres of the medium was sterilized in a fermenter vessel with a working capacity of 2 litres.

Fermentation in flasks: Triplicate sets of flasks containing the sterile medium at pH 5 were inoculated with 5% inoculum and incubated at R.T (28-33 C) for 5 days on a rotary shaker.

The biomass was harvested by filtering the contents of the flasks through Whatman No. 1 filter paper. The residue was washed repeatedly to remove any adhering N salts and dried at 80 C to a constant weight before analysis.

Pilot fermentation in fermentor: 75 ml of the pellet inoculum was added to the fermentor. The fermentation was carried out at 28-33 C for 5 days with agitation (200 rpm) and aeration at 0.66-1 vvm (volume of air per volume of medium per minute). 10 ml samples were drawn aseptically at 24 h intervals, centrifuged and the supernatant was preserved at -18 C. The precipitate was washed and dried at 80 C to a constant weight and analyzed.

Optimization of Culture Conditions for Protein Production

1. **Type and Size of Inoculum:** 3 ml and 5 ml each of the mycelial pellets and spore suspension with 10^7 spores/ml were used as inoculum in different flasks and incubated for 8 days.

2. **Effect of Aeration:** The fermentation was studied with continuous shaking, intermittent shaking for five minutes every two hours, on a rotary shaker (200 rpm) and with no shaking, for 8 days.
3. **Period of Incubation:** The fermentation flasks were incubated on a rotary shaker and incubation period was varied from one to eight days.
4. **Substrate Concentration:** The fermentation was studied with the initial substrate concentration varying from 0.5% to 3%, at 0.5% intervals.
5. **pH**: The H-ion concentration of the medium was adjusted to different pH values in the range 3.5 to 7 at 0.5 pH intervals.
6. **Nitrogen Sources:** N sources such as potassium nitrate, ammonium sulphate, ammonium chloride, diammonium hyrdrogen phosphate, urea, cattle urine and poultry droppings (extracts) were added to the basal medium in the concentration range of 250 to 600 mg/L. Nitrogen in cattle urine and poultry dropping extract was estimated by Kjeldahl method.
7. **All Optima Fermentation:** An all optima fermentation was studied with 1% of initial substrate concentration, 5% mycelial inoculum, in **T. virdie** medium (without peptone) with 350 mg N/L ammonium dihydrogen phosphate and incubation with continuous shaking on a rotary shaker for 5 days at 28-30 C.
8. **Mixed Cultures: 10% of** V/V of **Cellulomonas** sp. (Isolate B-54); **Saccharomyces cereviseae and Candida utilis** suspensions were added after 48 h incubation of flasks inoculated with **P. simplicissimum.**

Fermentation Studies in A Pilot Fermentor

The pH profile of the fermentation was determined with continuous aeration at 0.66 vvm and stirring at 200 rpm.

A batch fermentation with pH controlled at 5-5.5 with IN NaOH and continuous aeration and agiatation as above was carried out for 4 days.

A semicontinuous fermentation was studied with 20% of the biomass from the earlier batch retained in the fermentor. The pH was controlled between 5-5.5 and aeration and agitation were as mentioned above. The fermentation period was 5 days.

A mixed culture fermentation was studied by first using the fungal mycelial inoculum. After 36 h a washed culture of a 24 h old **Saccharomyces cerevisea** cultures which was growing in Potato broth in a shake flasks, made to a 10% suspension, was added to the fermentor, at a point where the reducing sugar as determined in the batch fermentation was maximum.

Samples drawn daily from the fermentations were analysed for reducing sugars in the supernatant and for crude protein in the precipitate.

Analysis: The solid matter consisting of unutilized substrate + fungal mycelia was analysed for dry matter yield and crude protein content.

The reducing sugars were determined by DNS method (Miller, 1959).

Results

Effect of Type and Size of Inoculum (Table 4.1, The 5% sporulated inoculum yielded a lower crude protein

(CP) and protein recovery of 22.3% and 14.4 g/100g substrate respectively after 8 days of incubation compared to 24.2% C.P. and 15.8 g/100 g PR with the 5% mycelial inoculum in 6 days. The lowest DMY was 645 mg/g and 598 mg/g substrate in the respective cases. An important feature observed was that the mycelial inoculum yielded a higher PR and CP within 6 days of incubation.

TABLE 4.1

Effect of Type and Size of Inoculum

Days of Incubation	*DMY mg/g substrate*	*CP %*	*PR g/100 g substrate*	*DMY mg/g*	*CP % substrate*	*PR g/100 g*
	Spore Suspension		3% Inoculum		Mycelial pellets	
Controls	1000	2.25	2.3	1000	2.40	2.4
2	942	2.8	2.6	921	4.2	3.9
4	895	5.9	5.3	823	10.1	8.3
6	782	13.6	10.6	687	10.9	11.6
8	704	15.3	10.8	658	17.5	11.5
	Spore Suspension		5% Inoculum		Mycelial pellets	
Control	1000	2.35	2.4	1000	2.60	2.6
2	931	3.1	2.9	908	7.1	6.4
4	880	7.6	6.7	794	193.9	13.8
6	724	16.8	12.2	652	24.2	15.8
8	645	22.3	14.4	598	19.8	11.8

The 3% inocula were sufficient in both cases as indicated by the lower yields of CP & PR. The DMY was however higher with 3% inocula than with 5% inocula.

Effect of Period of Incubation (Table 4.2, Fig. 4.23) with increasing period of incubation the CP content of the biomass increased upto 6 days. PR values declined after 5 days. The DMY and CP values for 5 days incubation were 680 mg/g and 24.4% respectively.

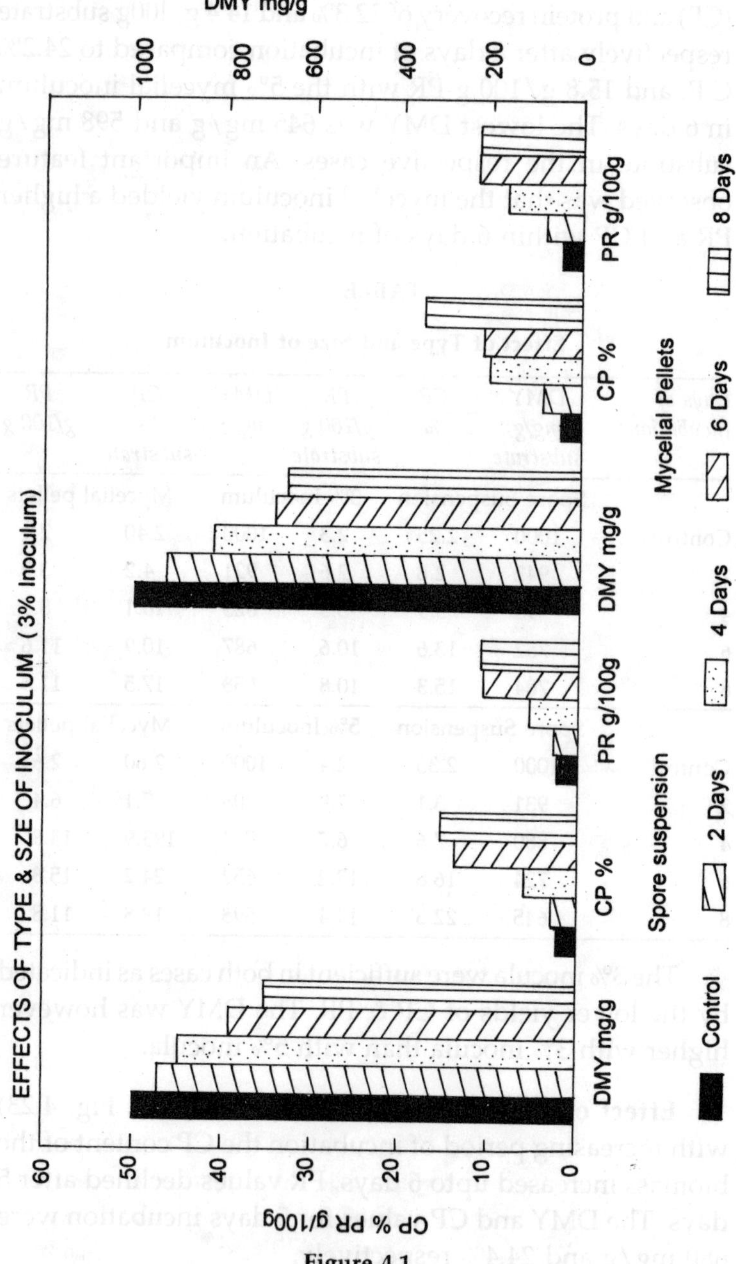
EFFECTS OF TYPE & SZE OF INOCULUM (3% Inoculum)
DMY mg/g
1000
800
600
400
200
0
CP % PR g/100g
60
50
40
30
20
10
0
DMY mg/g
CP %
PR g/100g
DMY mg/g
CP %
PR g/100g
Spore suspension
Mycelial Pellets
Control
2 Days
4 Days
6 Days
8 Days

Figure 4.1

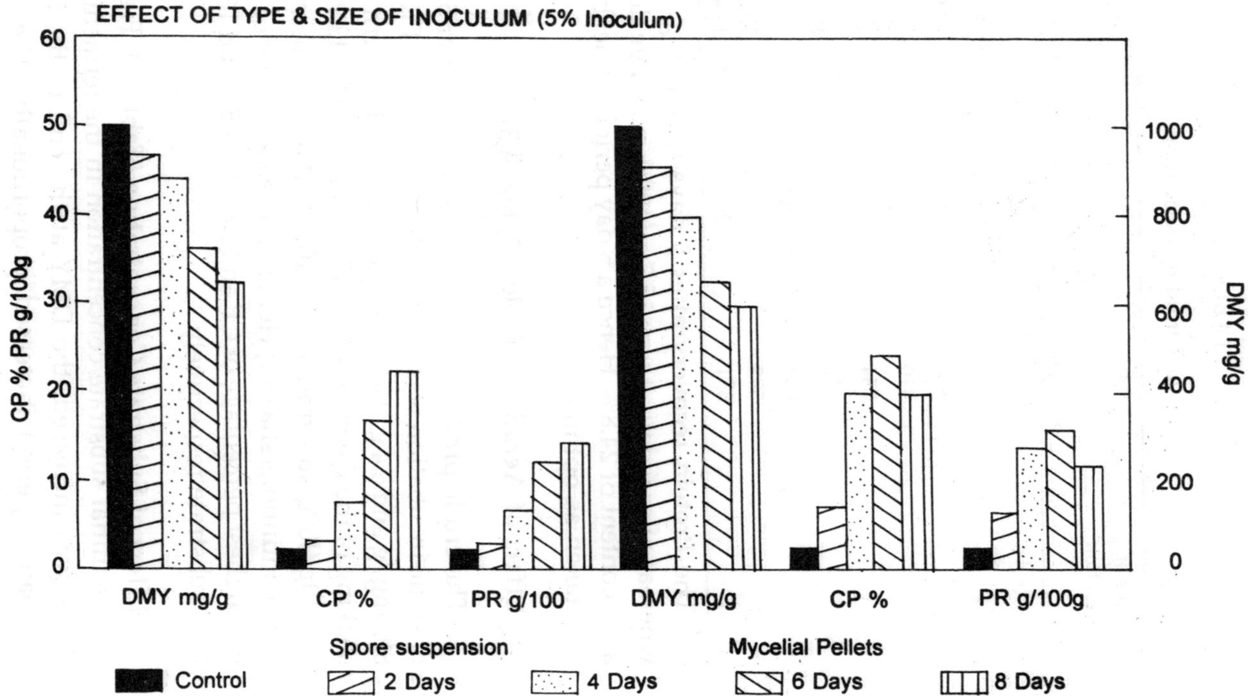

Figure 4.1 *contd...*

TABLE 4.2

Effect of Period of Incubation

Days of Incubation	*DMY mg/g substrate*	*CP %*	*PR g/100 g substrate*
Control	1000	2.5	2.5
1	984	3.2	3.1
2	875	8.9	7.8
3	810	16.7	13.5
4	734	21.3	15.6
5	680	24.4	16.6
6	634	24.8	15.7
7	593	21.6	15.2
8	571	20.0	11.4

The Protein recovery after 5 days was 16.6 g/100 g whereas after 6 days it was 15.7 g/100 g substrate despite a CP content of 24.8%. Hence a 5 day period of incubation was taken as optimum.

Effect of Aeration: (Table 4.3, Fig. 4.3)

The crude protein content of the biomass after 5 days of static incubation was 7.2% while the DMY and PR were 892 mg/g and 6.4 g/100 substrate respectively. Intermittent shaking of the flasks yielded 725 mg./g of DMY, 13.9% CP and 10g/100g substrate of PR after 5 days. Fermentation with continuous shaking yielded the least amount of DMY but highest percentage of CP and PR i.e. 24.5% and 16.5 g/100g substrate respectively.

Effect of Substrate Concentration (Table 4.4, Fig. 4.4) As the initial substrate concentration in the fermentation flasks was increased, the DMY at the end of the 5 day incubation period increased proportionally. The crude protein content was 25.2% with 0.5% substrate which

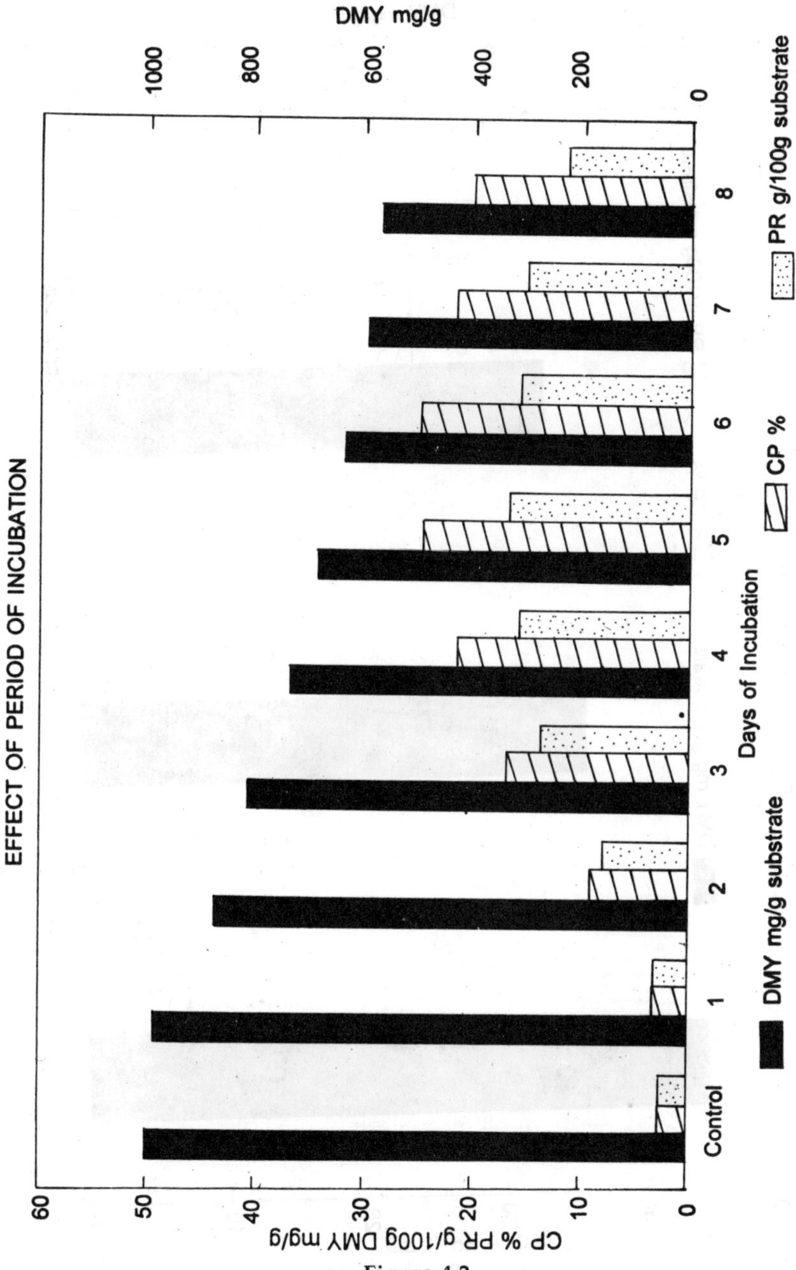
EFFECT OF PERIOD OF INCUBATION
DMY mg/g
0
200
400
600
800
1000
0
10
20
30
40
50
60
CP % PR g/100g DMY mg/g
Control
1
2
3
4
5
6
7
8
Days of Incubation
DMY mg/g substrate
CP %
PR g/100g substrate

Figure 4.2

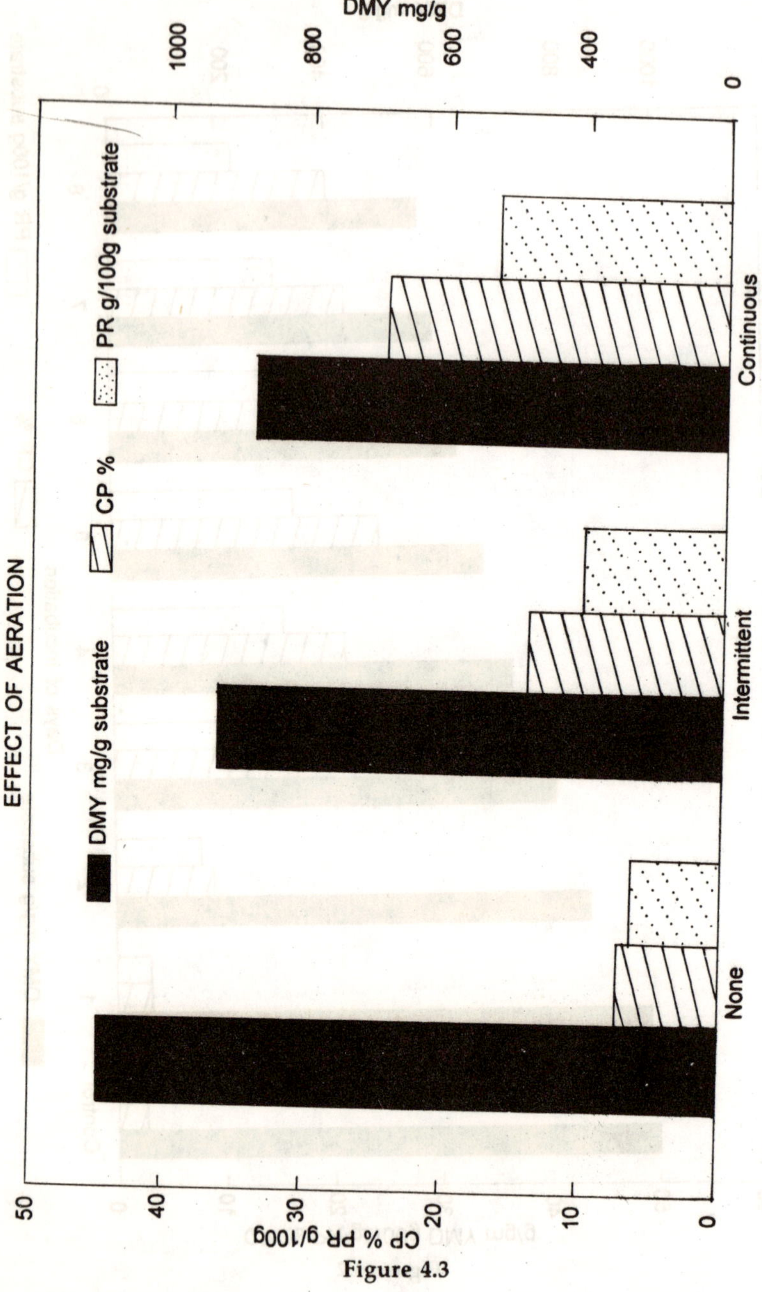
EFFECT OF AERATION
DMY mg/g substrate
CP %
PR g/100g substrate
DMY mg/g
1000
800
600
400
0
CP % PR g/100g
50
40
30
20
10
0
None
Intermittent
Continuous

Figure 4.3

however declined with a further increase in susbtrate concentration.

TABLE 4.3

Effect of Aeration

Extent of shaking	*DMY mg/g substrate*	*CP %*	*PR g/100g substrate*
None	892	7.2	6.4
Intermittent	725	13.9	10.0
Continuous	675	24.5	16.5

Table 4.4

Effect of Substrate Concentration

Concentration of Substrate g/100 ml	*DMY mg/g substrate*	*CP %*	*PR g/100g substrate*
0.5	658	25.2	16.6
1.0	665	24.6	16.4
1.5	676	20.3	13.7
2.0	695	18.3	12.7
2.5	704	12.4	8.7
3.07	27	10.3	7.5

However the PR/100g was 16.6 with 0.5% and 16.4 with 1% substrate concentration, which are very close values hence 0.5-1% substrate concentration was taken as the optimum for further studies.

Effect of pH: (Table 4.5, Fig. 4.5)

TABLE 4.5

Effect of pH

pH of medium	*DMY mg/g substrate*	*CP %*	*PR g/100g substrate*
3.5	684	19.5	13.3
4	680	20.6	14.0
4.5	674	22.9	15.4
5	671	24.7	16.6
5.5	673	24.5	16.5
6	675	21.6	14.6
6.5	679	20.2	13.7
7	682	16.4	11.2

The culture **P. simplicissimum** could be cultivated at all the variable H-ion concentration between 3.5-7 as indicated by the percentage of CP obtained. The overall protein recovery ranged from 11.2-16 g/100g. The optimum pH for protein production was in the range 5-5.5, as evident from the 24.7 and 24.5% protein content respectively. The DMY was 671 mg/g and 673 mg/g of substrate and the PR was 16.6 and 16.5 g/100g substrate with pH 5 and 5.5 respectively,

Effect of Nitrogen Sources (Table 4.6, Fig. 4.6)

Ammonium sulphate, yielded crude protein in the range 12.9 to 22.3 % which is low compared to other N sources like $NH_4H_3PO_4$, Urea or Poultry droppings, 350 mg N/L of ammonium sulphate was optimum.

Ammonium dihydrogen phosphate was the best N source among all those tested. It yielded a CP in the range 14.7-25.4% and PR between 10.8-181 g/100g substrate. The optimum concentration was 350 mg N/L.

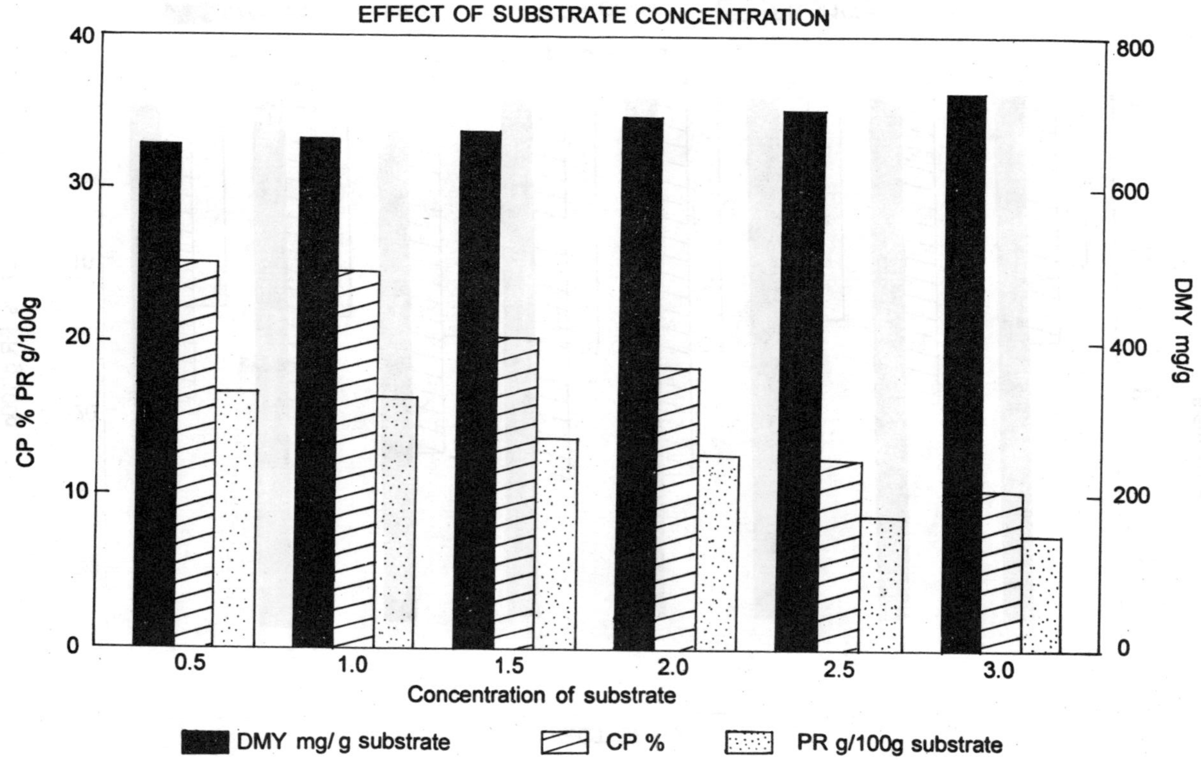
EFFECT OF SUBSTRATE CONCENTRATION
CP % PR g/100g
40
30
20
10
0
DMY mg/g
800
600
400
200
0
0.5
1.0
1.5
2.0
2.5
3.0
Concentration of substrate
DMY mg/ g substrate
CP %
PR g/100g substrate

Figure 4.4

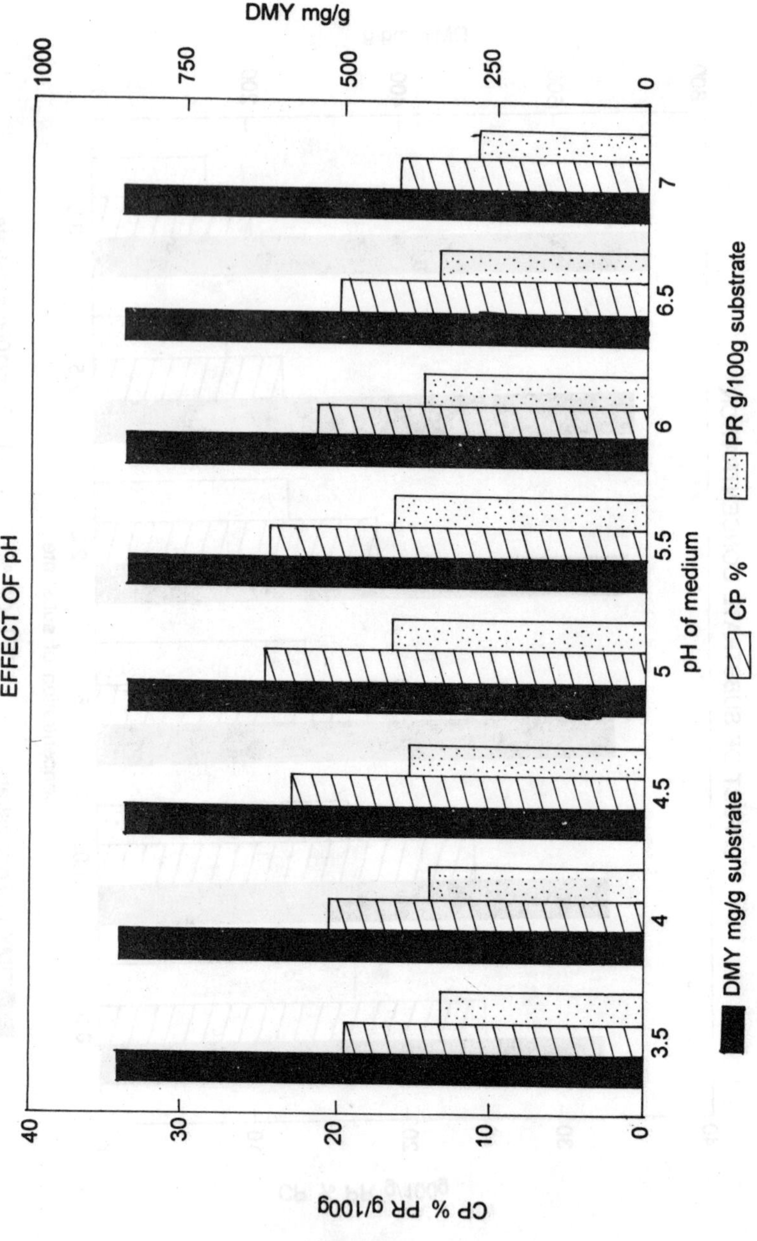
EFFECT OF pH
DMY mg/g
1000
750
500
250
0
40
30
20
10
0
CP % PR g/100g
3.5
4
4.5
5
5.5
6
6.5
7
pH of medium
DMY mg/g substrate
CP %
PR g/100g substrate

Figure 4.5

TABLE 4.6

Effect of Nitrogen Source

Concentration of N source mgN/L	*Ammonium sulphate*			*Ammonium dihydrogen phosphate*			*Potassium nitrate*		
	DMY mg/g substrate	*CP %*	*PR g/100g substrate*	*DMY mg/g substrate*	*CP %*	*PR g/100g substrate*	*DMY mg/g substrate*	*CP %*	*PR g/100g substrate*
250	731	12.9	9.4	728	19.9	14.5	740	12.4	9.2
300	726	15.4	11.2	719	24.5	17.7	735	14.1	10.4
350	714	22.3	15.9	712	25.4	18.1	728	20.6	15.0
400	709	21.6	15.3	710	24.8	17.1	716	23.3	16.7
450	717	20.8	14.9	718	22.7	16.3	719	22.4	16.1
500	720	19.0	13.7	725	17.3	12.5	726	21.6	15.7
600	726	15.4	11.2	734	14.7	10.8	741	15.5	11.5
	Urea			**Cattle Urine**			**Poultry Droppings**		
250	694	14.3	9.9	658	16.2	10.7	765	11.6	9.1
300	688	18.5	12.7	649	18.9	12.3	754	12.4	9.6
350	680	22.6	15.4	643	24.8	15.9	748	16.7	12.8
400	673	24.6	16.6	644	24.6	15.8	741	22.9	16.9
450	678	24.7	16.0	645	23.5	15.2	751	22.1	16.6
500	684	21.3	13.9	653	20.5	13.4	757	21.2	16.0
600	693	20.4	13.5	660	18.6	12.3	762	21.3	16.2

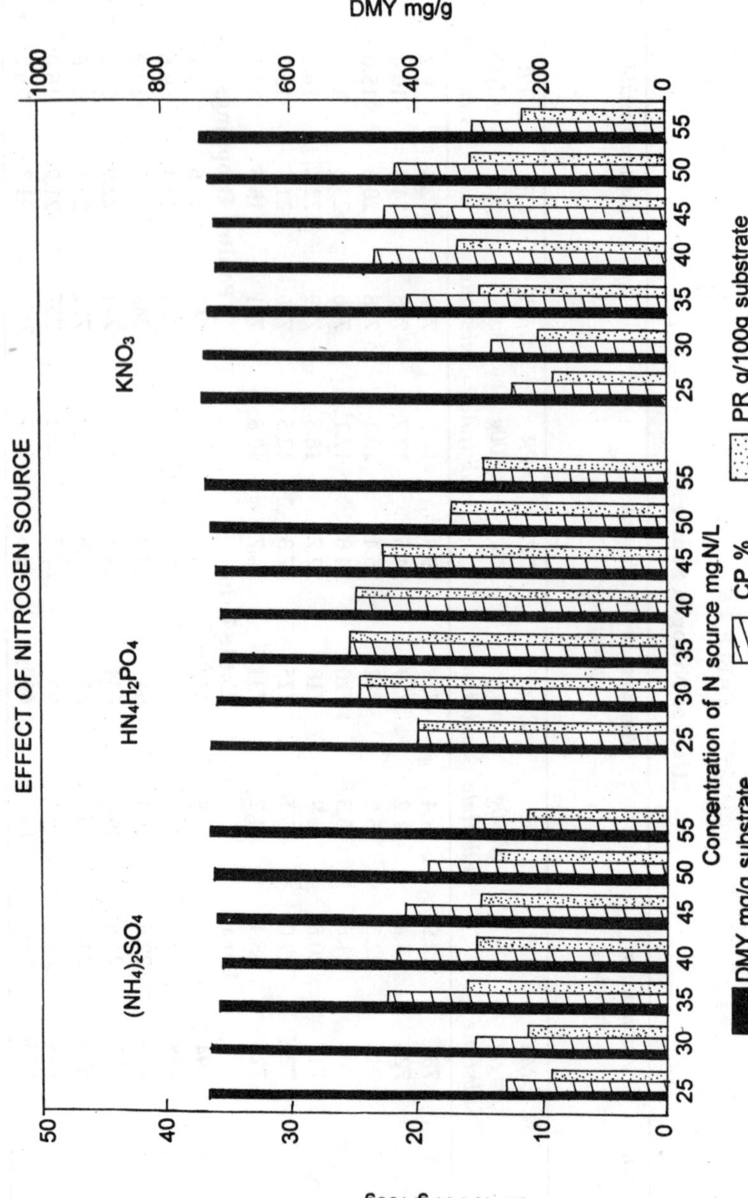
EFFECT OF NITROGEN SOURCE
DMY mg/g
0
200
400
600
800
1000
CP % PR g/100g
0
10
20
30
40
50
(NH4)2SO4
HN4H2PO4
KNO3
25
30
35
40
45
50
55
Concentration of N source mg N/L
DMY mg/g substrate
CP %
PR g/100g substrate

Figure 4.6

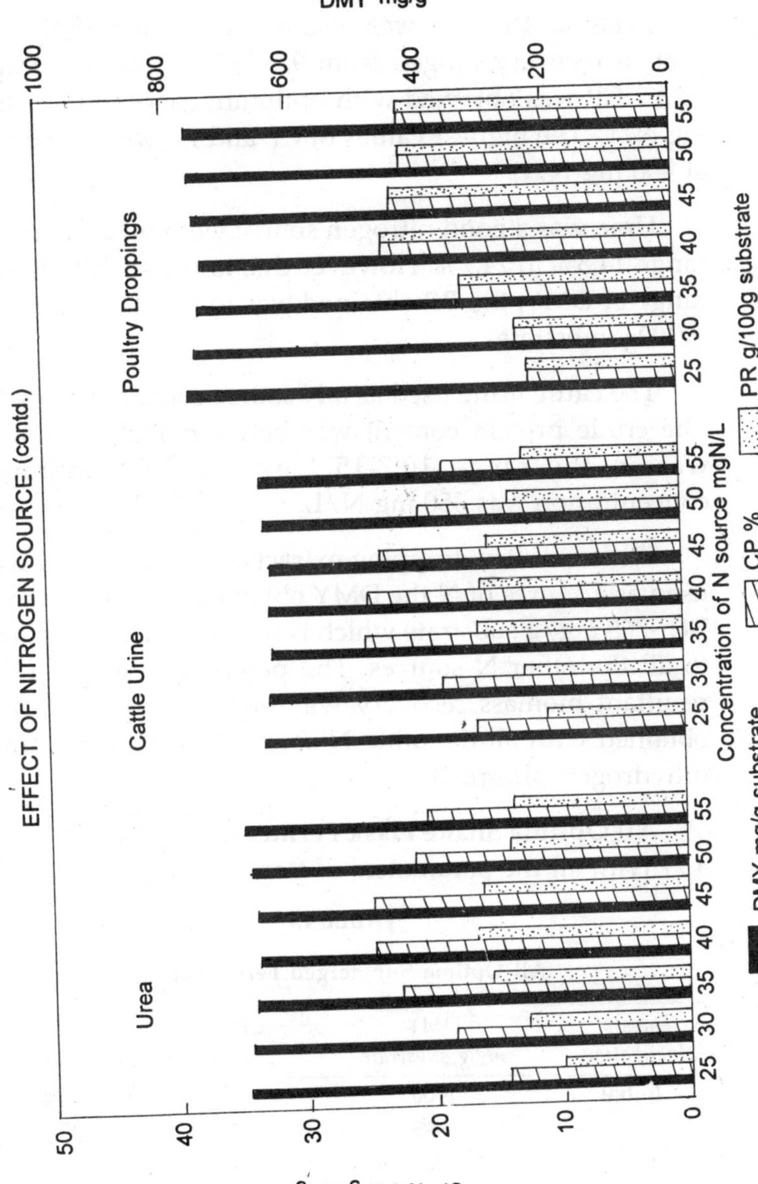

Figure 4.6 *(contd...)*

Potassium nitrate was also a poor source of N. The protein recovery ranged from 9.2-16.7 g/100g substrate. 23.3% CP was obtained with optimum concentration 400 mg N/L. The highest values of CP and PR were obtained at 400 mg N/L.

Urea was a good nitrogen source yielding a CP in the range 14.3% to 24.7%. However due to the slightly lower range of DMY, the PR obtained was in the range 9.9-16.6 g/100g substrate.

The cattle urine used as a N source contained 0.6% N. The crude protein content was between 16.2-24.8% and was in the range 10.7-15.9 g/100g. The optimum concentration was 350 mg N/L.

When poultry dropping extract containing 3% N was used as a source of N the DMY obtained was in the range 741 -765 mg/g substrate which is the highest as compared to all the other N sources. The percentage of CP in the resultant biomass recovery was higher than the values obtained with all the other N sources except ammonium dihydrogen phosphate.

All Optima Shake Flask Fermentation (Table 4.7, Fig. 4.7) With all the parameters of fermentation taken at

TABLE 4.7

All Optima Submerged Fermentation

Days of Incubation	*DMY mg/g substrate*	*CP %*	*PR G/100 substrate*
Initial	1000	2.4	2.4
1	985	2.5	2.5
2	912	8.6	7.8
3	841	16.2	13.6
4	774	24.2	18.7
5	680	28.5	19.4

TABLE 4.8

Effect of Mixed Culture Inoculum

Days of Incubation	*P. simplicissimum* + *Cellulomonas sp.*			*P. simplicissimum* + *C. utilis*			*P. simplicissimum* + *S. cerevisae*		
	DMY mg/g substrate	*CP %*	*PR g/100 g substrate*	*DMY mg/g substrate*	*CP %*	*PR g/100g substrate*	*DMY mg/g substrate*	*CP %*	*PR g/100g substrate*
Initial	1000	2.5	2.5	1000	2.4	2.4	1000	2.5	2.5
1	987	2.6	2.6	900	2.6	2.4	984	2.7	2.7
2	915	8.9	8.1	921	8.7	8.0	910	8.9	8.1
3	842	15.1	12.7	846	15.8	13.4	852	16.1	13.7
4	731	25.2	18.4	771	25.6	19.7	778	26.4	20.5
5	647	29.1	18.8	671	30.6	20.5	685	31.2	21.4

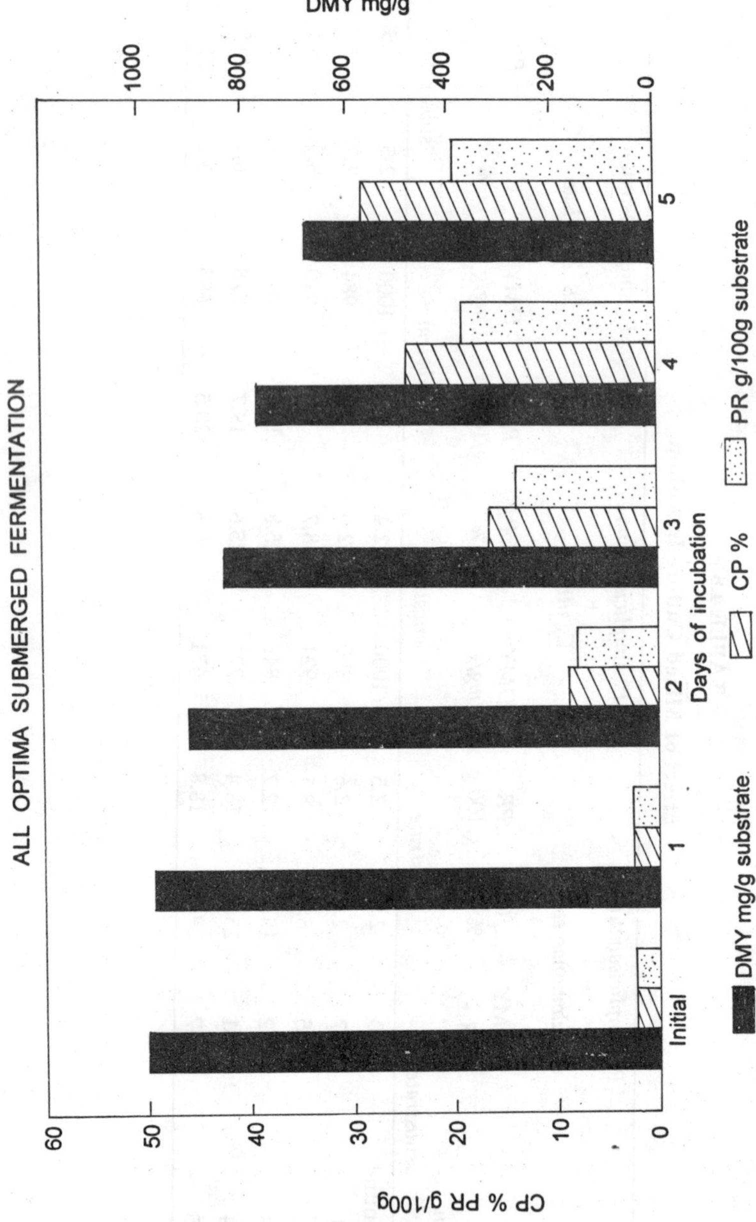
ALL OPTIMA SUBMERGED FERMENTATION
DMY mg/g
1000
800
600
400
200
0
60
50
40
30
20
10
0
CP % PR g/100g
Initial
1
2
3
4
5
Days of incubation
DMY mg/g substrate
CP %
PR g/100g substrate

Figure 4.7

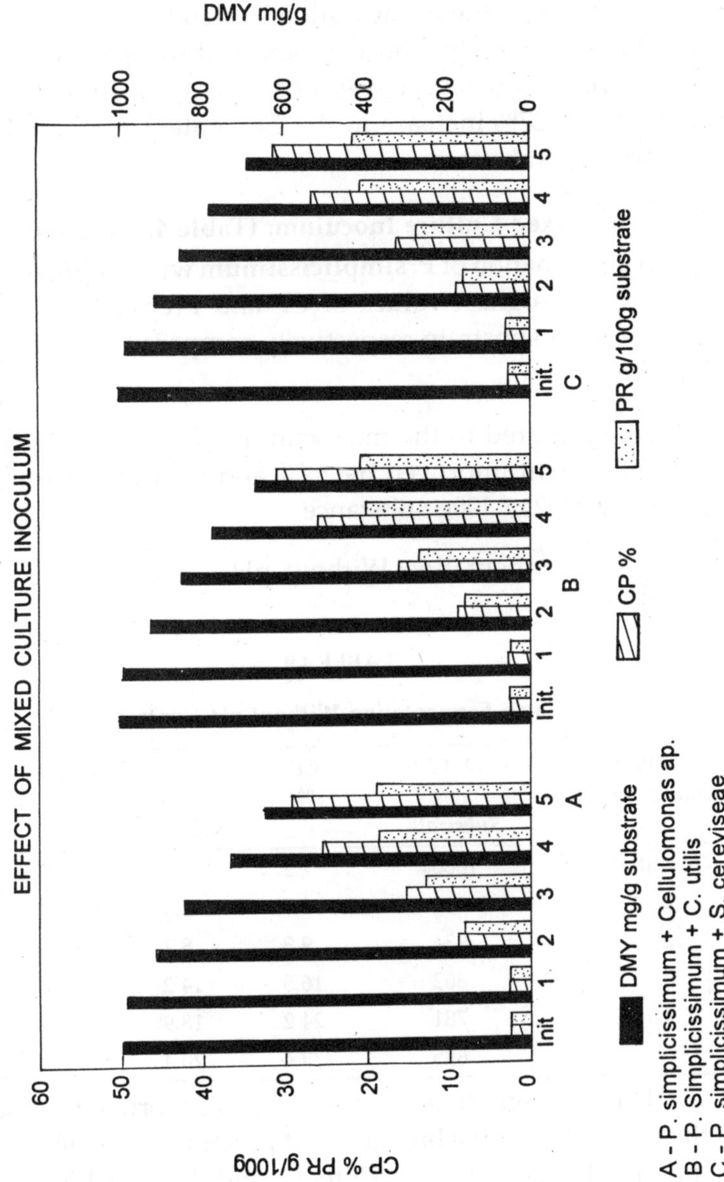

EFFECT OF MIXED CULTURE INOCULUM
DMY mg/g
1000
800
600
400
200
0
CP % PR g/100g
60
50
40
30
20
10
0
Init
1
2
3
4
5
A
Init.
1
2
3
4
5
B
Init.
1
2
3
4
5
C
DMY mg/g substrate
CP %
PR g/100g substrate
A - P. simplicissimum + Cellulomonas ap.
B - P. Simplicissimum + C. utilis
C - P. simplicissimum + S. cereviseae

Figure 4.8

optimum levels, the fermentation in shake flasks, yielded a DMY of 680 mg/g, and CP increased to 28.5% and the overall protein recovery was 19.4 g/100g substrate. Thus there was a 27% increase in the CP content compared to the original substrate.

Effect of Mixed Culture Inoculum: (Table 4.8, Fig. 4.8)

A combination of **P. simplicissimum** with **S. cereviseae** yielded the highest values of CP and PR i.e. 31.2% and 21.4 g/100 g substrate respectively compared to other co-cultures.

As compared to the monoculture (Table 4.7, Fig. 4.7) the CP content improved by 2.7% and the overall protein recovery by 2g/ 100g substance.

Batch Fermentation Without pH Control (Table 4.9, Fig. 4.9).

TABLE 4.9

Batch Fermentation Without pH Control

Days Incubation	*DMY mg/g Substrate*	*CP %*	*PR g/100g Substrate*	*PH*
Initial	1000	2.2	2.2	5.5
1	980	2.4	2.4	4.5
2	934	9.3	8.7	4.1
3	862	16.5	14.2	4.2
4	781	24.2	18.9	4.1
5	695	29.4	20.4	4.1

This fermentation was performed in order to study the pH profile of the biomass and protein production. The initial pH declined from 5.5 to 4.5 and then further to 4.1 in two days, after which it stabilized at 4.2-4.1 till the end of the fermentation period. In this scale up process, without pH control the CP content was 29.4% and the final protein recovery was 20.4 g/100g substrate.

Batch Fermentation With pH Controlled at 5-5.5
Table 4.10, fig. 4.10

TABLE 4.10

Batch Fermentation With 5-5.5

Days of Incubation	*DMY mg/g substrate*	*CP %*	*PR g/100 g substrate*	*Reducing sugar mg/ml*
Initial	1000	2.2	2.2	0.15
1	984	2.3	2.3	3.34
2	941	9.8	9.2	4.85
3	833	18.1	15.1	0.81
4	721	25.3	18.2	0.43
5	685	31.2	21.4	0.44

The effect of pH control on the yield of protein as also formation of reducing sugar content in the fermentation broth at various times was determined as a guideline for the time of inoculation of the second culture in a mixed culture fermentation.

At the end of five days the CP content of the biomass increased to 31.2%. As a result the net protein recovery was 21.4% g/100g substrate indicating a 1% increased over the fermentation without pH control.

The reducing sugar content in the fermentation broth was 0.15 mg/ml at the start. It increased to 3.34 mg/ml after 2 days and 4.85 mg/ml after 3 days of incubation, after which it declined sharply.

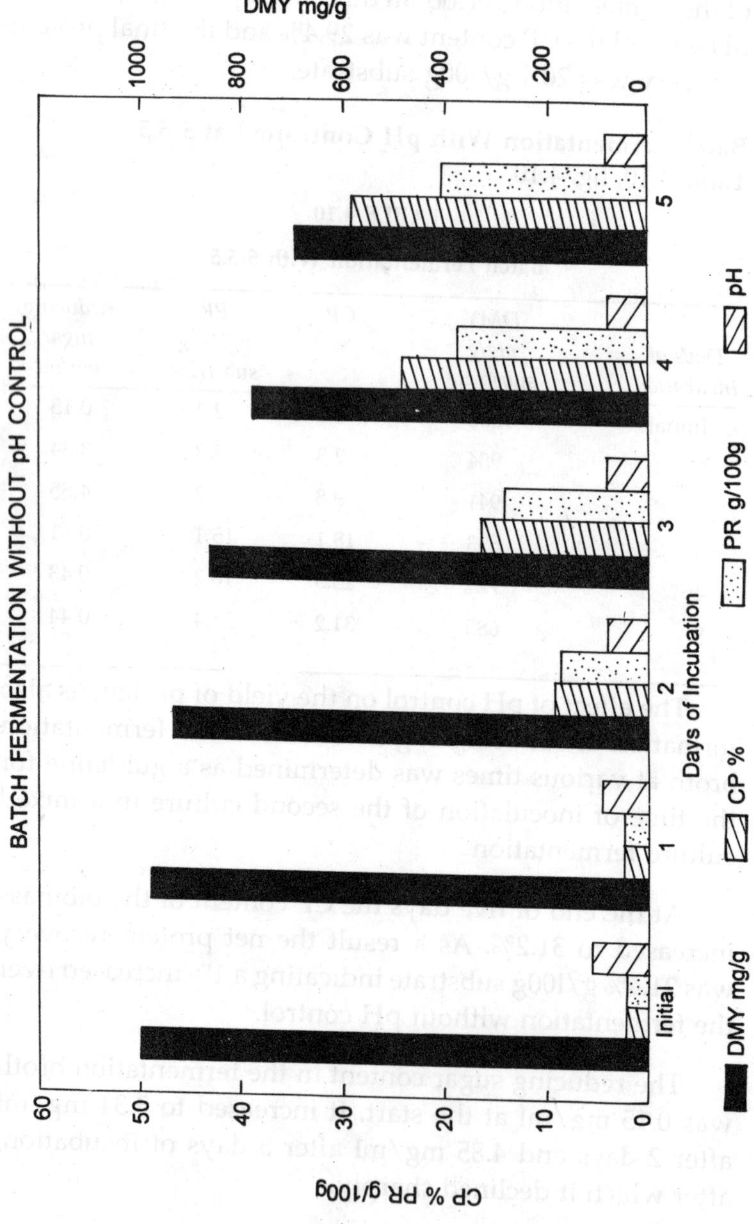
BATCH FERMENTATION WITHOUT pH CONTROL
DMY mg/g
1000
800
600
400
200
0
CP % PR g/100g
60
50
40
30
20
10
0
Initial
1
2
3
4
5
Days of Incubation
DMY mg/g
CP %
PR g/100g
pH

Figure 4.9

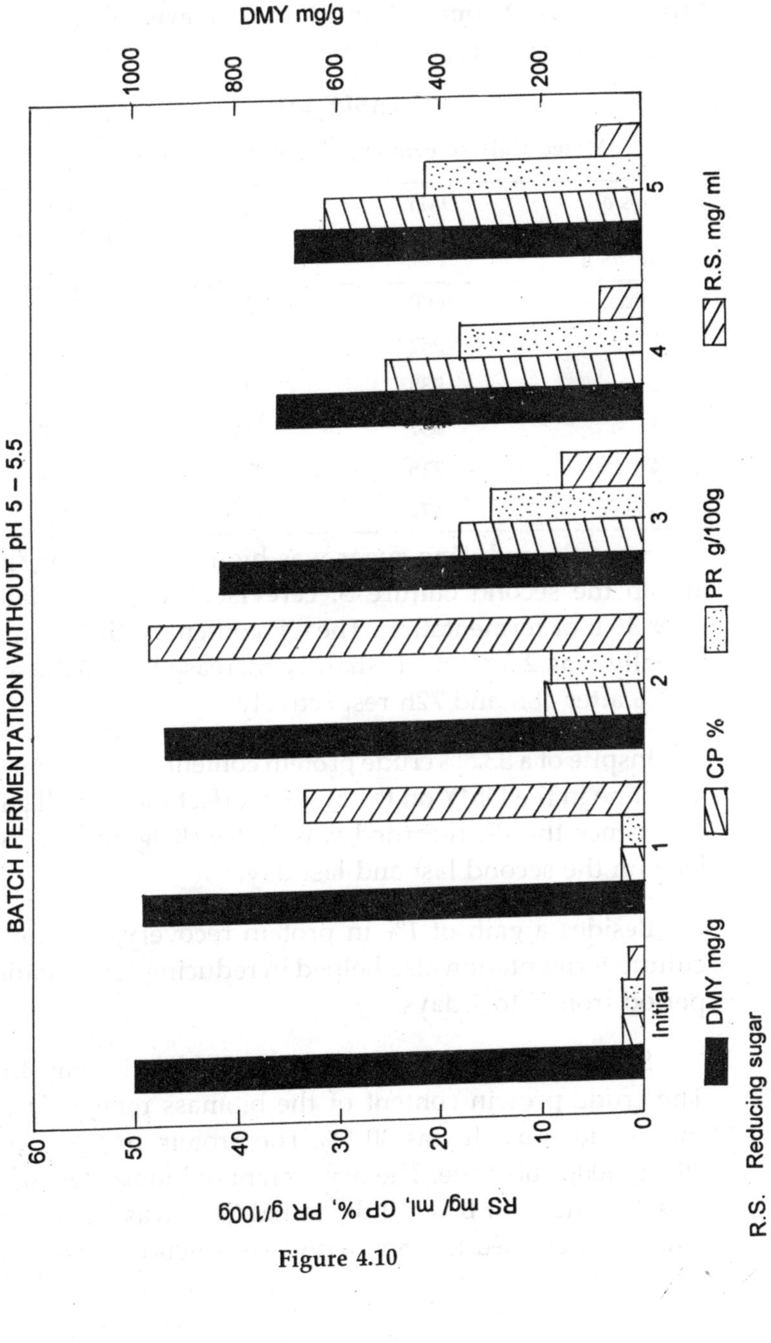

Figure 4.10

Mixed Culture Fermentation (With S. cereviseae) (Table 4.11, Fig. 4.11)

TABLE 4.11

Mixed Culture Fermentation (with S. cereviseae)

Days of of Incubation	*DMY mg/g substrate*	*CP%* —	*PR g/100 substrate*
Initial	1000	2.2	2.2
1	982	2.3	2.3
2	938	13.2	12.4
3	831	23.7	19.7
4	715	27.9	22.1
5	671	33.5	22.5

Since the reducing sugar was highest at 4.85 mg/ml, at 48h the second culture **S. cereviseae** was inoculated after 36 h of fermentation. The CP content of the biomass initially was 2.3% which sharply increased to 13.2% and 23.7% after 48h and 72h respectively.

Inspite of a 33.5% crude protein content in the biomass, a decline in the DMY on the 5th day offset the overall gain and hence the PR recorded was 22.1 g/100g and 22.5 g/100g on the second last and last day.

Besides a gain of 1% in protein recovery, the mixed culture fermentation also helped in reducing fermentation period from 5 to 4 days.

Semi continuous Fermentation (Table 4.12, Fig. 4.12) The crude protein content of the biomass retained from the previous batch was 30.1%. The protein recovery was 20.6 g/100g substrate. The dry weight of biomass retained was 1368 mg. For batch II the initial CP% was 5.2%. After 1 day, it increased to 6.8%, with a conspicuous absence of

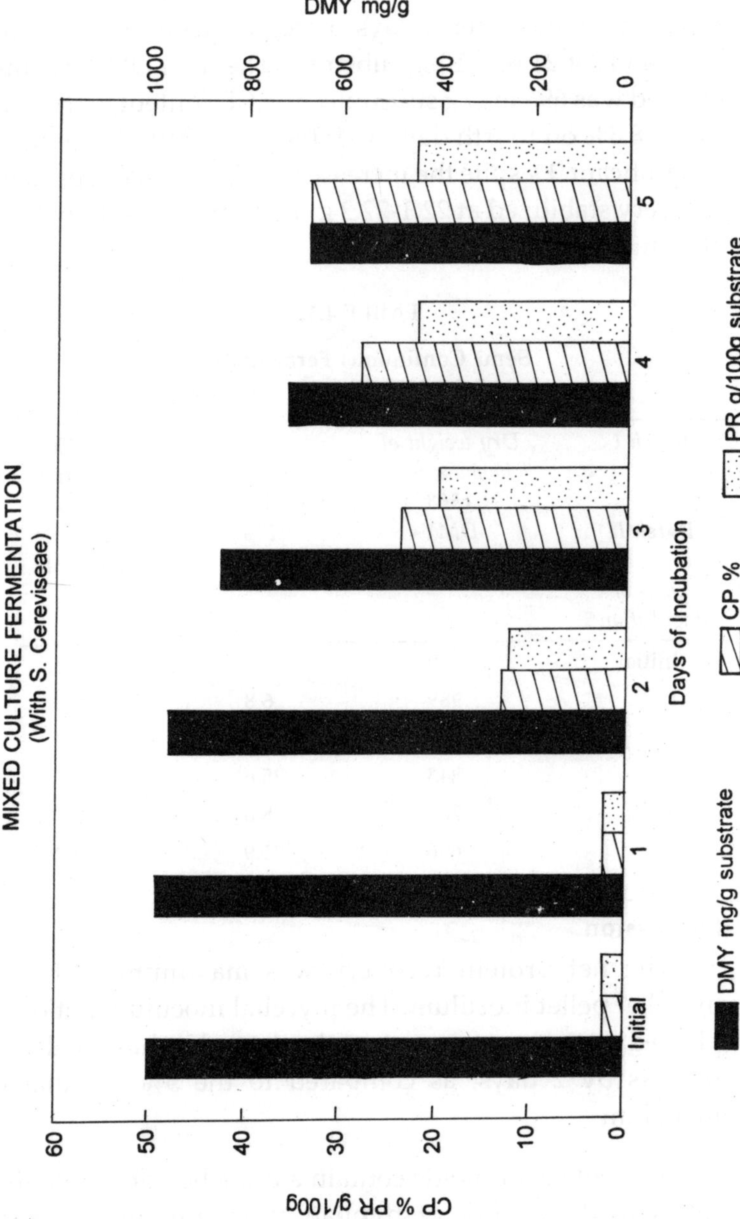
MIXED CULTURE FERMENTATION
(With S. Cereviseae)
DMY mg/g
1000
800
600
400
200
0
CP % PR g/100g
60
50
40
30
20
10
0
Initial
1
2
3
4
5
Days of Incubation
DMY mg/g substrate
CP %
PR g/100g substrate

Figure 4.11

a lag phase and after 2 days it sharply rose to 18.1 % to yield a PR of 21.6g/ 100g substrate. The final DMY by this method was 696 mg/g substrate. The CP content increased from 28.8% on fourth day to 31.9% on the fifth day, which is significant. Despite the increase in CP, the overall protein recovery stabilized at 22.1-22.2 g/100g on the last two days of fermentation.

TABLE 4.12

Semi Continuous Fermentation
(pH 5-5.5,20% Biomass Retained)

Batch I	*Dry weight of biomass mg.*	*CP%*	*PRg/100g substrate*
	1368	*30.1*	*20.6*
Batch II	*DMY mg/g -substrate*	*CP%*	*PRg/100g substrate*
Days of Incubation			
Initial	1000	5.2	5.2
1	989	6.8	6.7
2	989	6.8	6.7
3	843	25.6	21.6
4	767	28.8	22.1
5	696	31.9	22.2

Discussion

The net protein recovery was maximum with 5% mycelial pellet inoculum. The mycelial inoculum not only yielded better protein recoveries but also hastened the process by 2 days, as compared to the 5% sporulated inoculum.

The pellets of molds contain a branched and partially interwined network of hyphae and with this form of inoculum, the sparged air was adequate for mixing. Ek &

SEMI CONTINUOUS FERMENTATION
(pH 5-5.5, 20% Biomass Retained)
DMY mg/g
1000
800
600
400
200
0
CP % PR g/100g
60
50
40
30
20
10
0
Initial
1
2
3
4
5
Days of incubation
DMY mg/g substrate
CP %
PR g/100g substrate

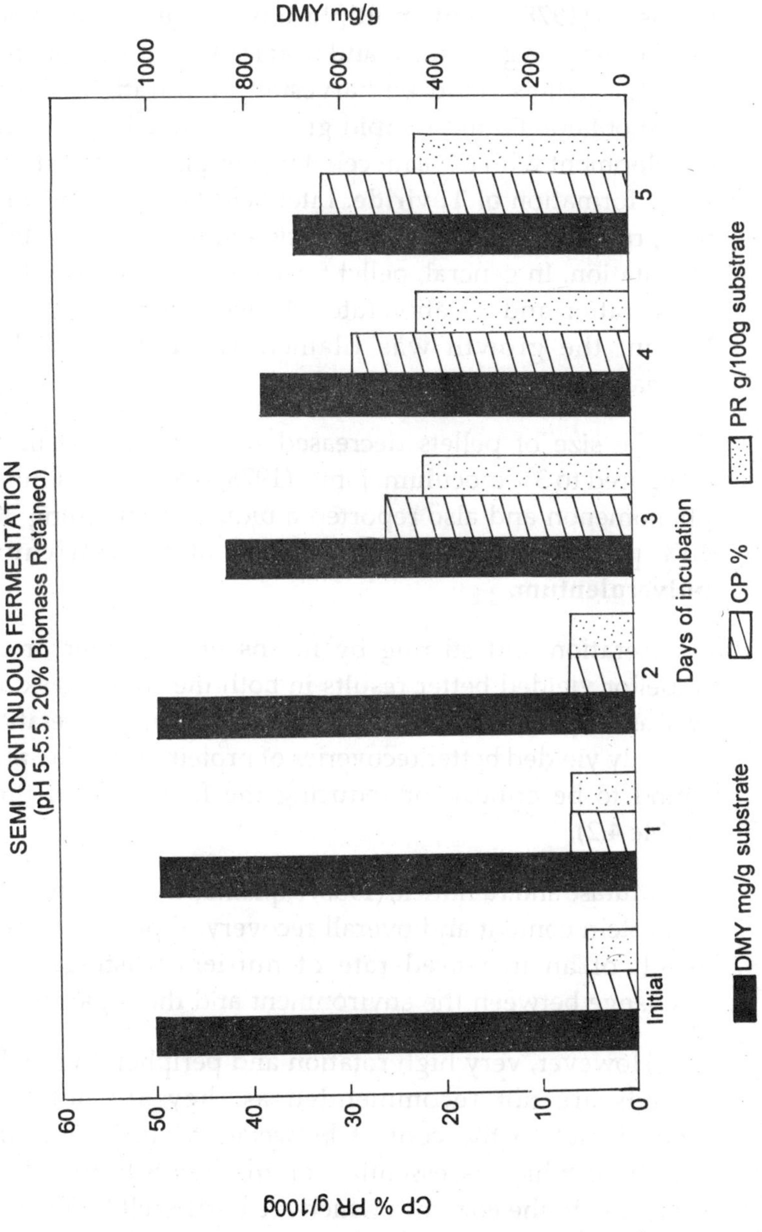

Figure 4.12

Eriksson (1978) cited multiple advantages of such an inoculum viz. a good mass and heat transport and mixing; also, the pellets could be harvested by filtration. Ghose (1978) obtained a more rapid growth and earlier enzyme development with a 5% mycelial inoculum, compared to a spore formation of **T. viride.** Litchfield (1979) found that the formation of pellets is largely determined by the extent of agitation. In general, pellet formation was favoured by low aeration and agitation rates. Above 1.15 mM Oxygen/ L/min, the growth was filamentous and the yields decreased.

The size of pellets decreased with 5% inoculum as compared to 3% inoculum. Janus (1978) observed a similar phenomenon and also reported a biomass containing 30-40% protein with pellet inoculum of **Sporotrichum pulverulentum.**

Aeration and stirring by means of a sparger or an impellor yielded better results in both the shake flask, as well as the pilot fermentor experiments. Stirring and aeration not only yielded better recoveries of proteins but were also found to be critical for reducing the fermentation time (Table 4.2).

Murase and Kendrick, (1986) explained a similar increase in protein content and overall recovery of protein to be a result of an increased rate of nutrient-waste-gaseous exchange between the environment and the organism.

However, very high rotation and peripheral impellor speeds are not recommended as they are not only detrimental to the contact between the organism and substrate which is essential for the accessibility of the substrate to the enzymes which are partly cell bound, but are also damaging to the fungal mycelia.

As indicated by Table 4.3, the overall protein recovery increased with the incubation time till 5 days, after which the rate of increasing protein was very slow. Hence, an incubation for 5 days was optimum.

In case of filamentous organisms, growth occurs by terminal extension of hyphae and not by binary fission. Improper shaking and extended time of incubation may therefore lead to formation of heavy masses of mold mycelia or may cause sporulation. Dhillon et al. (1982) found a period of seven days incubation to be sufficient for fermentation of wheat straw. Srinivasan et al. (1983) recommended a rapid harvesting of biomass before the differentiation or sporulation of the molds occurred and the growth turned green in colour due to the release of spores.

Shaker et al. (1984) determined a 4 day incubation period to be critical for high protein recovery and also suggested that increased holding time would result in increasing costs of operation.

Table 4.4 indicates a low protein and high dry matter yield with more than 1% substrate concentration. This is probably because of the fact that above % concentration, the milled rumen ingesta with a high bulk density, forms a slurry which prevents proper mixing and aeration. The low crude protein values may also be due to exhaustion of nutrients other than energy sources and an increase in pH which may be inhibitory for the growth of cells as also the induction of the cellulolytic enzyme synthesis. Wang et al. (1979) proposed other reasons like toxic or inhibitory effects of specific compounds on key enzymes or other structural cell components for substrate inhibitions.

Maximum working cellulose concentrations reported

are about 2% in small laboratory fermentors, although Nystrom and Deluca (1978) used 8% cellulose in a slurry form which approached the solid or **koji** type of fermentation. Garg & and Neelkantan (1982 a) and Shaker et al. (1984) obtained similar low yields with more than 1% substrate concentration.

The results of the variables of the initial H-ion concentration of the medium (Table 4.5) show that the culture of P. **simplicissimum** can tolerate as well as grow in the studied range of pH 3.5-7. pH 5-5.5 was however, found to be optimum for protein production. Lower yields of protein at adverse pH conditions may be due to the fact that being proteins, enzymes undergo changes in solubility, osmotic pressure, viscosity and ionisation of attached amino and carboxyl groups, as the pH of their medium changes. It is likely that the changes in enzyme activity with pH reflect changes in ionisation of enzymes or enzyme — substrate complex.

A wide range of pH tolerance has been reported by Singh and Kalra (1978), Garg and Neelkantan (1981) and Dhillon et al. (1982). The CP content was found to be maximum at pH 4 while the maximum cellulase activity was between pH 4 to 6, and net protein recovery was maximum at pH 4 and pH 7 in case **of Aspergillus terreus** GN1 (Garg & Neelkantan, 1981).

Armstrong and Martin (1983) suggested the selection of an optimal pH such that it is a compromise between the optimum for enzyme stability, cellulolysis and growth of an organism. Rao et al. (1983) indicated a wide range of pH tolerance by the organism **Penicillium janthinellum** since the maximum growth was obtained at pH 3, 5 and 7.

N is usually the next most plentiful substance in the

fermentation media after the C source (Litchfield et al., 1963). Bearing in mind the possible rural and farm level operation of the process, it was necessary to search for new and cheaper N sources to replace peptone. Suitable N sources from biomass productions generally include ammonia, ammonium salts, nitrates, urea and animal wastes. The N should be in sufficient quantity to meet the growth requirements of the microorganism. It is important to maintain the C : N ratio in the range of 10:1 or less which favours high cell protein content and minimizes accumulation of lipids or cell storage substances (Litchfield, 1985).

However, as the N concentration was increased beyond the optimum level, a steady decline in the protein content was observed. When ammonium N is used as N source, pH tends to fall because N is assimilated, and H^+ is left in the medium. However with NO_3^- to NH_3 and the pH tends to rise. In case of organic NH_4^+ Compounds also, pH tends to rise (Litchfield et al., 1963). In the Present studies ammonium dihydrogen phosphate was found to be much superior to other sources such as potassium nitrate. In an attempt to replace peptone and other protein hydrolysates, animal wastes like cattle urine and poultry droppings were used. The N component in urine is composed of 50.3-74.2% Urea N, 4.0-6.4% allantoin N and 0.3-0.6% ammonia N. It also contains 1.15% Potassium, 0.05% Sodium, 0.34% Calcium and 0.02% Magnesium (Hutton et al., 1965). Poultry excreta is another rich source of both N and P as well as other major and minor elements. It contains 5 to 7% Nitrogen and 4 to 6% Phosphorous (Gaur et al., 1984).

All the organic sources of N studied were found to be optimum at 350/400 mg N/L. The failure of ammonium sulphate to give better yeilds despite the efficiency of the other ammonium compounds as a N source is not understood. The SO_4^{2} may have some adverse effect. Among the organic N sources, poultry dropping extract was found to give better yields of protein. Factors such as those mentioned above and other unknown factors may have stimulatory effects. The lower efficiency of urea and cattle urine is probably because of the rapid change in pH, which may be detrimental for protein production.

To summarise, ammonium dihydrogen phosphate at 350 mg N/L and poultry droppings at 400 mg N/L were recorded as ideal N sources. The possible explanation for this is that Phosphorous may be a limiting nutrient in the medium and it may have been supplied in adequate concentration by both these diverse sources of N. Another probable reason is that the phosphate molecule may have contributed to the buffering capacity of the medium, where the sulphate molecule had failed.

The overall results are not in corroboration with those obtained by Shukla and Dutta (1965), Singh and Kalra (1978) who found nitrate N to be more efficient than Ammonia N for yielding higher amounts of crude protein. Singh and Kalra, (1978) also found higher concentrations of N sources like Urea to be toxic due to accumulation of ammonium ions released.

Garg and Neelkantan (1982b) concluded that **Aspergillus terreus** GNI utilized inorganic ammonium N sources less efficiently than organic N sources. Ghate (1984) found ammonium nitrate to be the best source of N for **Aspergillus niger** and many other cellulolytic fungi.

The efficiency of ammonium dihydrogen phosphate is in agreement with the results obtained by Dhillon et al. (1982), who found that 0.5 g N/L of ammonium dihydrogen phosphate increased the CP content of the biomass of

Myrothecium verrucaria five fold, the highest in comparison with other N sources. Neelkantan (1987) found 7.5% poultry excreta extract to be an efficient N source for **Neurospora sitophila.**

In an all-optima shake-flask fermentation the yield of protein was 19.4g/100g substrate, though the CP was 28.5%. The DMY was 680 mg/g substrate. The dry matter loss is essentially and totally due to the decomposition of carbohydrates. The greater the carbohydrate fraction, the greater is the loss in weight (Griffin et al., 1975). The crude protein content of the biomass is comparable to that reported by Singh and Kalra (1978) who obtained a 28.12% protein content with **M. verrucaria** on corn cobs, Dhillon et al., (1980) who reported 30.5% crude protein on cellulose fractions and Rao et al., (1983) who obtained 30% CP in a final biomass from alkali treated, autoclaved and washed straw.

Smith et al. (1975) have reported a higher CP% in the biomass **of Aspergillus oryzae** CMI 44242 on ground barley. Romantschuk and Lehtomaki (1978) obtained a biomass with 55% CP from **Paecilomyces variotii** on sulphite waste liquor, Ivarson & Morita, (1982) reported a yield of 45% CP with **Scytalidium acidophilum** grown on waste paper.

Anderson and Solomons (1983) reported a record yield of 60% CP with **Fusarium graminearum** CMI 145425 on glucose.

Scale-up Fermentation In a Pilot Fermentor

In the scale up process, fermentation was carried out in a pilot fermentor with aeration at 0.66 vvm and agitation at 200 rpm. However, higher impellor speed was not considered useful as it led to foaming, splashing and overflowing, leading to loss of dry matter. Many authors have found that moderate agitation accelerates the breakdown of cellulose though excessive agitation causes a reduction in hydrolysis rate. This was due to the detachment of organisms and the substrate fibre, shear stress and deactivation of the gas liquid interface in the fermentor (EK and Erikson, 1978; Mukatak et al., 1983; Murase and Kendrick, 1986). Excess aeration also often leads to poor growth, perhaps due to too rapid removal of CO_2 (Solomons, 1985).

The study of the pH profile of the fermentation showed that as the fermentation proceeded into the logarithmic phase, the pH rapidly decreased (Table 4.9).

The scale up process, accompanied by aeration and stirring improved the CP% and protein recovery by a marginal 1 %. The failure to obtain a better yield may be attributed to the fall in the pH or product inhibition (Howell and Stuck, 1975).

A similar fall in pH was reported during the metabolism of cellulose by Mandels et al., (1975) and Peitersen (1975c). This fall was associated with the disappearance of sugar. Thus the conditions for maximum cellulase production were observed to be different from conditions for optimum growth.

However, when the pH was controlled, at 5 -5.5 with NaOH, the scale-up process was accompanied by an increase in the CP content and protein recoveries. The CP content recorded was 31.2%, which is higher by 2.7% than the CP of shake flask biomass and the overall protein recovery improved by 2g/100g substrate. Peitersen (1975a) obtained a 21.25% CP content after a 9 day incubation period, with 0.05% - 0.1% peptone in the medium, in a 5 liter fermentor.

In order to remove celiobiose, which is inhibitory to cellulase activity, if present in high concentration, a second culture S. **cereviseae** which was cellobiase positive was utilized in a mixed culture fermentation (Table 4.11). The time of inoculation was chosen such that it preceded the period of maximum saccharification of cellulose i.e. at 36h. The final CP content increased rapidly to 33.5% and the protein recovery improved to 22.5%/100g, which is about 1% improvement over the yields of the monoculture.

The moderate increase in the protein recoveries may be attributed to (1) the low DMY of yeast culture compared to fungi and (2) to the pH and other environmental conditions, including the available concentration of N which may not be conducive to a better protein yield by the yeast.

However, a positive trait observed was that the time required for peak-up was reduced by one day, which was most probably due to faster growth rate of yeast as also its scavenging action on celiobiose and other sugars.

Similar marginal improvement in the yield and also hastening of the process by 24 to 48h with mixed culture was reported by Peitersen (1975b) and Sarkar and Prabhu (1982). Peitersen (1975c) however obtained no improvement in the yield.

Semicontinuous method of fermentation of lignocellulosics has not been well studied. In the present studies when 20% of the biomass was retained, the CP% of the biomass in the second batch improved from 30.1 % to 31.9%. Besides the 1.8% gain in CP and 1.6% gain in overall protein recovery, the fermentation period was shortened by 12-24h. Srinivasan et al. (1983) have reported a 1.4 - 1.6% improvement in the CP content of the biomass, by the semi-continuous method.

Hence, the minimum period required for fermentation of rumen ingesta was 4 days, either by mixed culture or semicontinuous fermentations.

In the scale up process the DMY was in the range of 671-695 mg/g and the CP content of the biomass ranged from 29.4 - 33.5%. The mixed culture fermentation yielded maximum CP in the biomass.

The overall protein recovery ranged from 20.4 to 22.5%. On an average 22-23 g/100g PR was recorded by mixed culture and semi-continuous fermentation in 4 days, thereby yielding a better protein productivity per volume per hour than batch fermentation.

5

Solid Substrate Fermentation

A solid substrate fermentation is one in which the substrate is not suspended in water but is in an almost solid condition. Though SSF is a traditional process it has been only recently modernised and standardized to produce enzymes, food and feeds from agricultural wastes (Toyoma, 1976).

SSF of lignocellulosics is a polyfactorial process with a limited number of control possibilities (Zadrazil, 1983; Laukevics et al., 1984).

Straw of various crops like rice, wheat or barley have been fermented by SSF using filamentous fungi or yeasts in different types of fermentation vessels like cement mixers (Han et al., 1976 a, b: Hesseltine, 1977), petridishes (Kokke, 1977), tumble fermentors (Ghai et al., 1980; Prendergast et al., 1983), reactors with 4 horizontal perforated plates on a vertical cylinder (Rosen & Schugerl, 1983) or in trays stacked on each other (Ulmer, 1983).

Rhodes and Orton (1975) and Hesseltine (1977) reported SSF of feedlot wastes in 2 litre flasks incubated with a tilt or in horizontal drums while Ulmer et al., (1981) fermented feed lot wastes in cylindrical jars.

Raimbault et al., (1977) and Senez et al., (1980) reported protein enrichment of starchy wastes from cassava and other sources in a bread making blender.

Supplementation of agricultural forestry wastes with fertilizer mixes or animal manure and urine has been studied by Moo Young (1979b), Ranjhan (1980), Viesturs et al. (1981), Neelkantan (1987) and Gupta (1988).

Materials and Methods

Microorganism: the fungal isolate M-21 identified as **Penicillium simplicissimum** was cultivated and maintained as described earlier.

Inocolum: The inoculum with 0.5 g/ml of mycelia was prepared as described in Chapter 4 and used in the SSF.

Substrate: Hammermilled rumen ingesta treated with 5% NaOH and autoclaved, was used as a substrate. The pH was adjusted to 5 with dilute acid. 100 g of the dry substrate was loosely filled into trays (30 x 40 × 6 cm) or petridishes (15 cm dia. x 2 cm), to a depth of 10 to 12 mm. These plates/trays could be stacked on each other as in mushroom cultivation, so that they occupied relatively less space.

Culture Medium: A high salt solution (Potassium dihydrogen phosphate - 2g, ammonium sulphate - 1.4 g, urea - 0.35g, made to a volume of 500 ml with tap water) was formulated. The required volume was sprinkled on the substrate after sterilization.

Procedure: 10 ml of inoculum was evenly spread on the substrate. The substrate, culture medium and the inoculum were mixed thoroughly with a spatula, and plates/trays were stacked into a humidified incubator with an aeration device which released water vapour saturated air at the rate of 8L/h. The plates were incubated at 30 ± 1 C for 7 days. The contents were mixed daily with the help of a wooden spatula. After the necessary incubation period, the residual biomass was dried and analyzed for DMY, CP and PR as described in chapter 4.

Optimization of Fermentation Parameters

1. **Pretreatment of Substrate** : Rumen ingesta which was either roughly chopped to 1 cm size, hammermilled to 1 mm size or hammermilled + 5% NaOH (autoclave) treated was taken as substrate.
2. **Sterilization of substrate** : 5% NaOH (autoclave) treated samples which gave highest protein production were heated at 70 C for 30 min *(quasi* pasteurization) or autoclaved at 121.6C for 20 min or left with no sterilization, before being used as substrates.
3. **Period of Incubation** : The fermentation period was varied from 2 to 7 days.
4. **Initial Moisture Content** : The initial moisture content of substrate, after addition of high salt solution and inoculum was adjusted to 45%, 60% and 75% with distilled water whenever necessary.
5. **Aeration** : The SSF trays were incubated either with no aeration in the humidifed incubator or aeration with water vapour situated air at 8 L/h.
6. **Nitrogen sources** 50% of the Nitrogen in the high salt solution was replaced with $(NH_4)_2SO_4$, $NH_4H_2PO_4$, cattle urine or poultry droppings. The total concentration of N in the medium was however maintained at 3.5 g N/L, as in the earlier high salt solution.

7. **All Optima Fermentation**: An all optima SSF was studied with 100g hammermilled + 5% NaOH treated substrate, 3.5g N/L of N in the form of $(NH_4)_2SO_4$ and poultry droppings, (50 : 50), 60% initial moisture content and aeration at the rate of 8 L/h of water vapour saturated air and 5 days of incubation period.

Results

Effects of Pretreatment: (Table 5.1, Fig. 5.1). The DMY ranged from 925 to 870 mg/g substrate, with all the three pretreatment variables.

TABLE 5.1

Effect of Pretreatment

Type of Pretreatment	*DMY mg/g substrate*	*CP %*	*PR g/100g substrate*
Chopped	925	8.5	7.9
Hammermilled	898	13.0	11.7
Milled, 5% NaOH (AC)	870	20.3	17.7

The CP was maximum i.e. 20.3% with the delignified substrate and so also the protein recovery which was 17g/100g showing more than a two fold increase as compared to the roughly chopped substrate.

Effect of Sterilization of Substrate : (Table 5.2, Fig. 5.2) The DM yields with all the variables of sterilization were in a narrow range of 871-888 mg/g substrate.

The range of CP% of the biomass obtained was also very narrow, 16.6 to 20.4%, both the heat treatments yielded almost similar amount of CP%. The autoclaved substrate yielded 17.8 g/ 100g of protein recovery and the pasteurized substrate yielded 17.7 g/100 g. Thus compared to the 14.7 g/100 g PR with non sterile substrate there was almost a 3g/100g improvement with either of the treatments.

TABLE 5.2

Effect of Sterilization of Substrate

Temp& Time of Sterilization	*DMY mg/g substrate*	*CP %*	*PR g/100g substrate*
121.6C, 20 min.	871	20.4	17.8
70 C, 30 min.	873	20.3	17.7
None	888	16.6	14.7

Effect of Period of Incubation: (Table 5.3, Fig. 5.3) The DMY at the end of six and seven days was 881 mg/g substrate respectively. The CP was 20.2% and 20.3% respectively and the PR which was 17.8g/100g after 6 days decreased slightly to 17.6g/100g after 7 days. Though the values of CP were almost similar on the 6th and 7th day, because of the slightly better protein recoveries and consideration of the time factor, the incubation period of six days was taken as optimum.

Effect of Initial Moisture Content: (Table 5.4, Fig. 5.4). The DMY did not vary very widely with the change in the initial moisture content of the substrate. It was between 872 - 887 mg/g substrate. The CP however was affected by deficiency or excess of moisture as 45% moisture yielded 18.3% CP, 75% moisture yielded 15.3% CP while 60% moisture yielded 20.2% CP. The PR was similarly lowest 13.3g/100g with 75% moisture, 16.2g/100g with 45% moisture and highest 17.8g/100g substrate with 60% moisture.

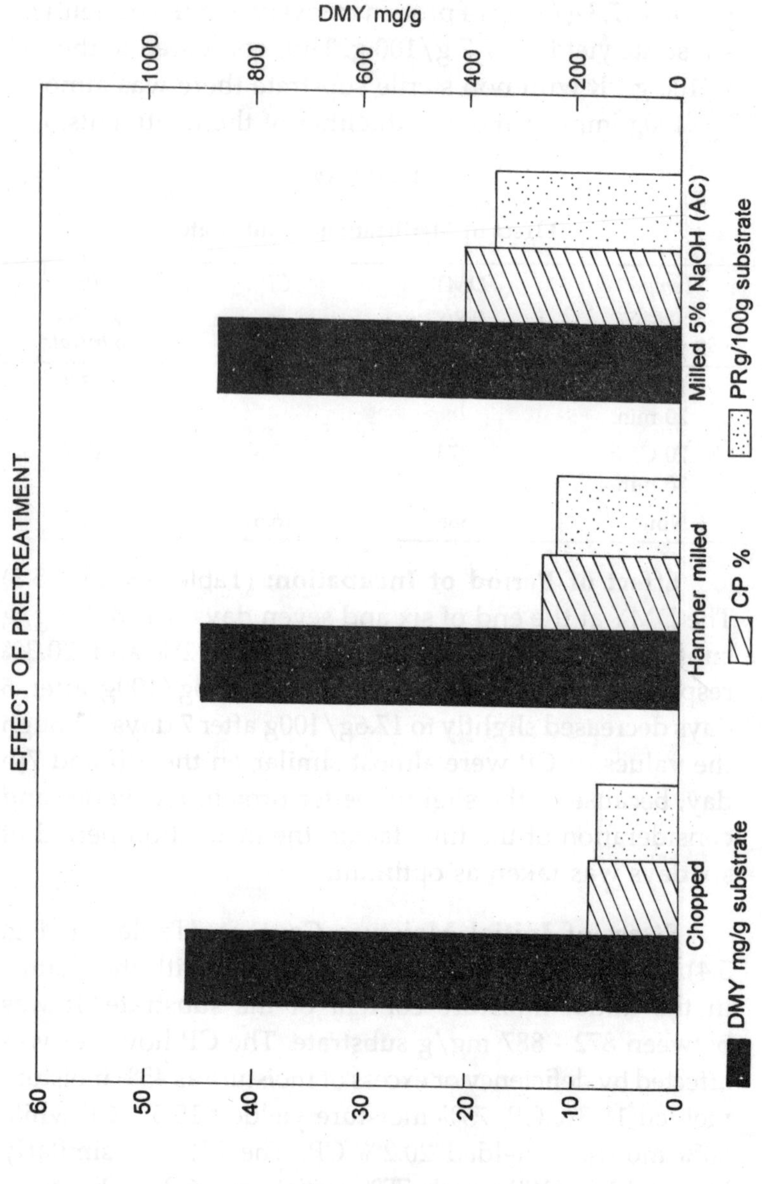
EFFECT OF PRETREATMENT
DMY mg/g
0
200
400
600
800
1000
CP % PR g/100g
0
10
20
30
40
50
60
Chopped
Hammer milled
Milled 5% NaOH (AC)
DMY mg/g substrate
CP %
PR g/100g substrate

Figure 5.1

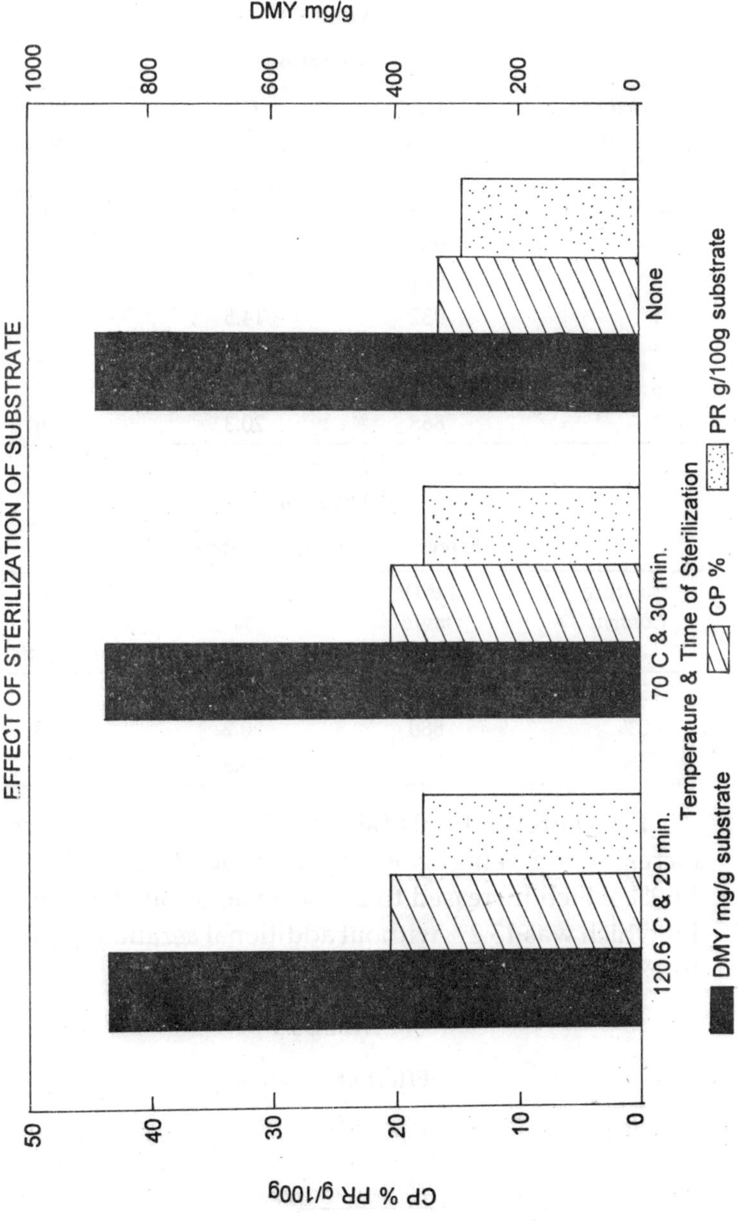
EFFECT OF STERILIZATION OF SUBSTRATE
DMY mg/g
1000
800
600
400
200
0
CP % PR g/100g
50
40
30
20
10
0
120.6 C & 20 min.
70 C & 30 min.
None
Temperature & Time of Sterilization
DMY mg/g substrate
CP %
PR g/100g substrate

Figure 5.2

TABLE 5.3

Effect of Incubation Period

Period of Incubation (days)	*DMY mg/g substrate*	*CP %*	*PR g/100g substrate*
Control	1000	3.5	3.5
2	981	6.5	6.4
3	964	9.8	9.4
4	932	14.5	13.5
5	915	17.6	16.1
6	881	20.2	17.8
7	868	20.3	17.6

TABLE 5.4

Effect of Moisture Content

Moisture Content	*DMY mg/g substrate*	*CP %*	*PR g/100g substrate*
45%	887	18.3	16.2
60%	880	20.2	17.8
75%	872	15.3	13.3

Effect of Aeration: (Table 5.5, Fig. 5.5) substrate which increased to 864 mg/g on additional aeration. The CP was 14.9% which increased to 20.4% on aeration at 8 L/h. The PR which was 13.2% without additional aeration improved to 17. 6% with 8 L/h aeration.

TABLE 5.5

Effect of Aeration

Aeration	*DMY mg/g substrate*	*CP %*	*PR g/100g substrate*
8L/h	864	20.4	17.6
None	885	14.9	13.2

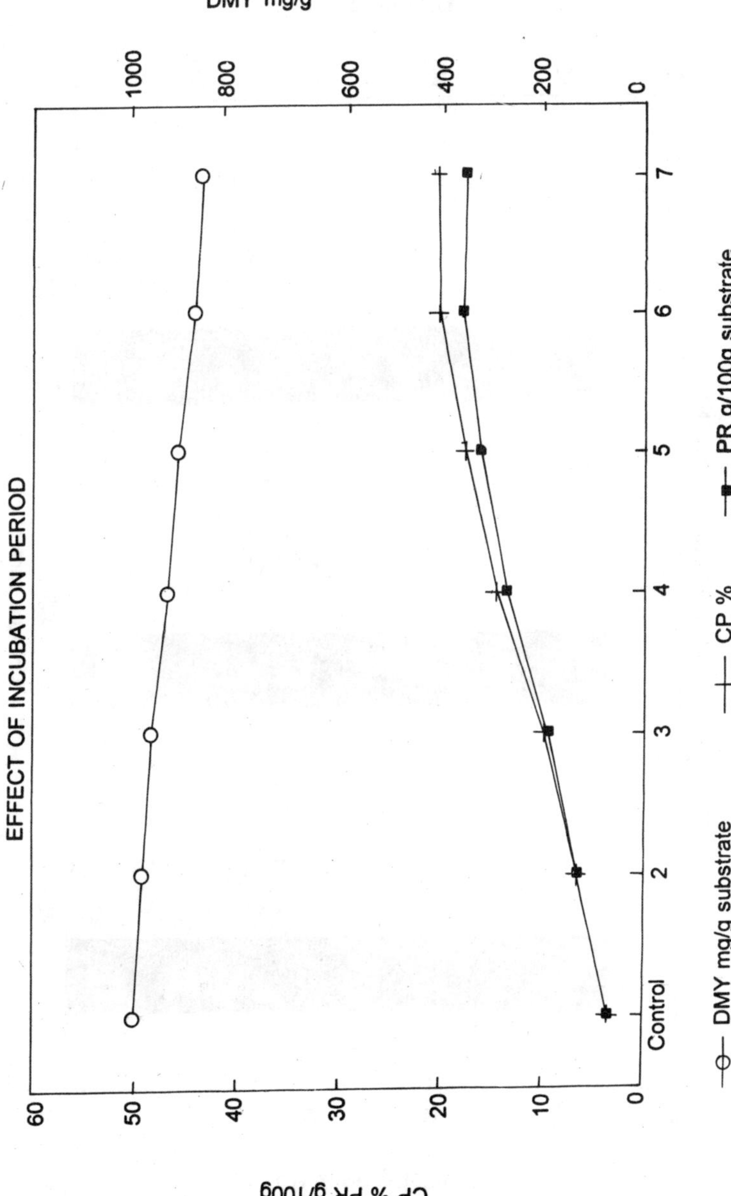
EFFECT OF INCUBATION PERIOD
DMY mg/g
CP % PR g/100g
1000
800
600
400
200
0
60
50
40
30
20
10
0
Control
2
3
4
5
6
7
DMY mg/g substrate
CP %
PR g/100g substrate

Figure 5.3

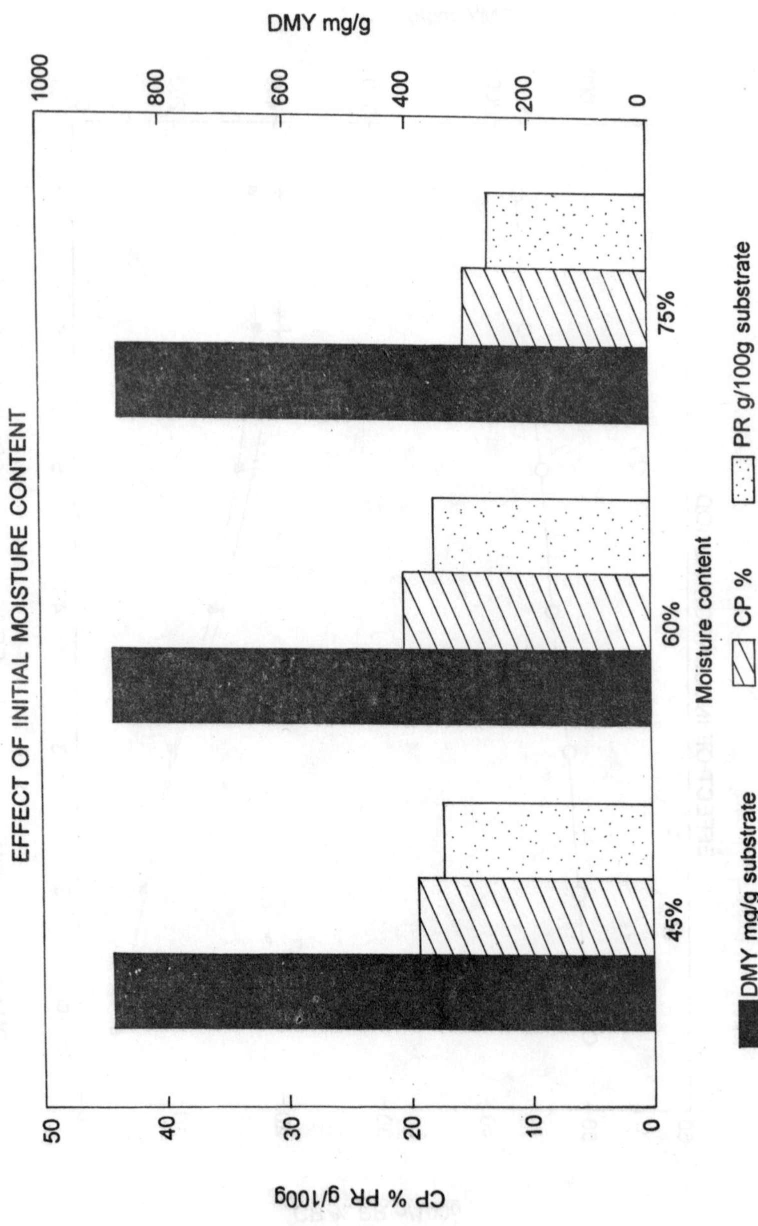
EFFECT OF INITIAL MOISTURE CONTENT
DMY mg/g
1000
800
600
400
200
0
CP % PR g/100g
50
40
30
20
10
0
45%
60%
75%
Moisture content
DMY mg/g substrate
CP %
PR g/100g substrate

Figure 5.4

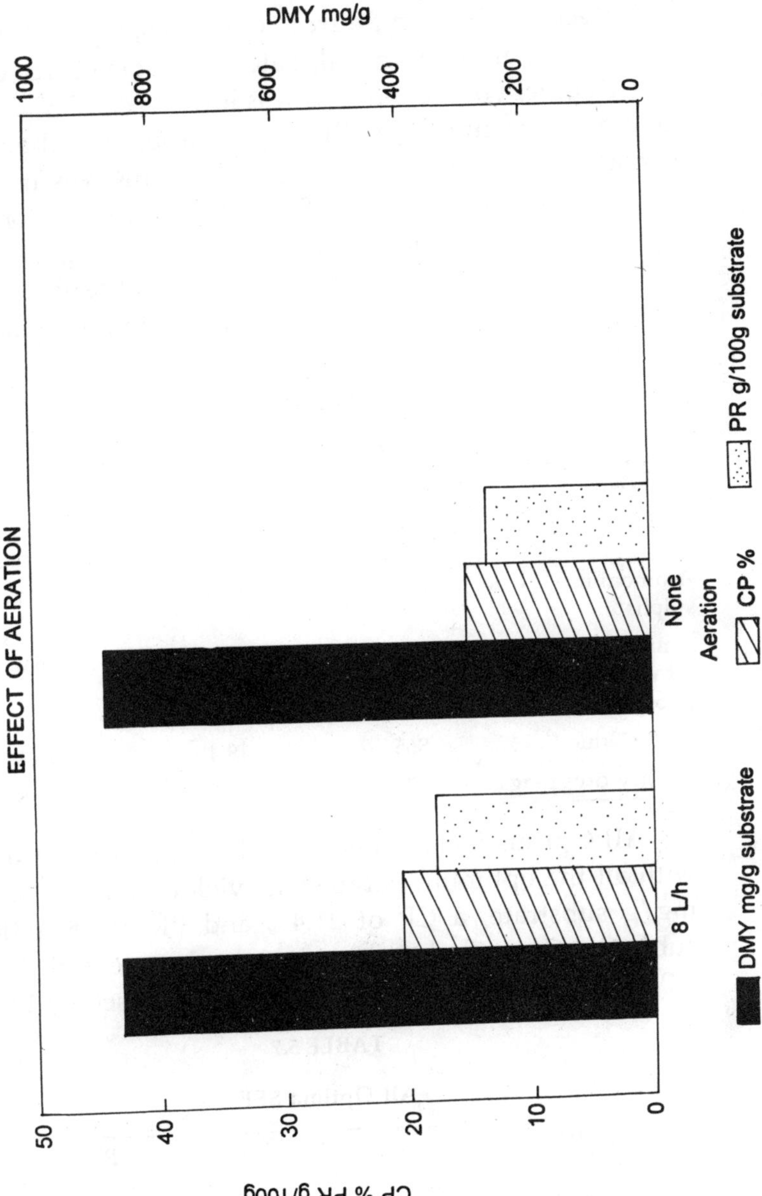
EFFECT OF AERATION
DMY mg/g
1000
800
600
400
200
0
CP % PR g/100g
50
40
30
20
10
0
8 L/h
None
Aeration
DMY mg/g substrate
CP %
PR g/100g substrate

Figure 5.5

Effect of Nitrogen Source : (Table 5.6, Fig. 5.6). With 3.5 g N/L of ammonium sulphate as the sole source of N, the CP content of the biomass was lowest i.e., 17.3%. With 50% replacement of N with poultry droppings, the CP% increased to a maximum of 20.3%. The PR was highest with poultry droppings i.e., 17.8g/100g, whereas ammonium sulphate by itself yielded a PR of 15.2g/100g. A 50% replacement with ammonium hydrogen phosphate and cattle urine yielded a small increase to 16.6 and 16.8 g protein per 100 g substrate.

TABLE 5.6

Effect of Nitrogen Source

50% N replacement	*DMY mg/g substrate*	*CP %*	*PR g/100g substrate*
Ammonium sulphate	881	17.3	15.2
Ammonium dihydrogen phosphate	870	19.1	16.6
Cattle Urine	865	19.4	16.8
Poultry droppings	877	20.3	17.8

All Optima SSF : (Table 5.7). The SSF of the substrate with all the optimum parameters, yielded a DMY of 876 mg/g substrate, a CP of 21.4% and PR of 18.7g/100g substrate. Compared to the original substrate with 1.57% CP, the protein content of the biomass increased by 19.8%.

TABLE 5.7

All Optima SSF

DMY mg/g substrate	*CP %*	*PR g/100g substrate*
876	21.4	18.77

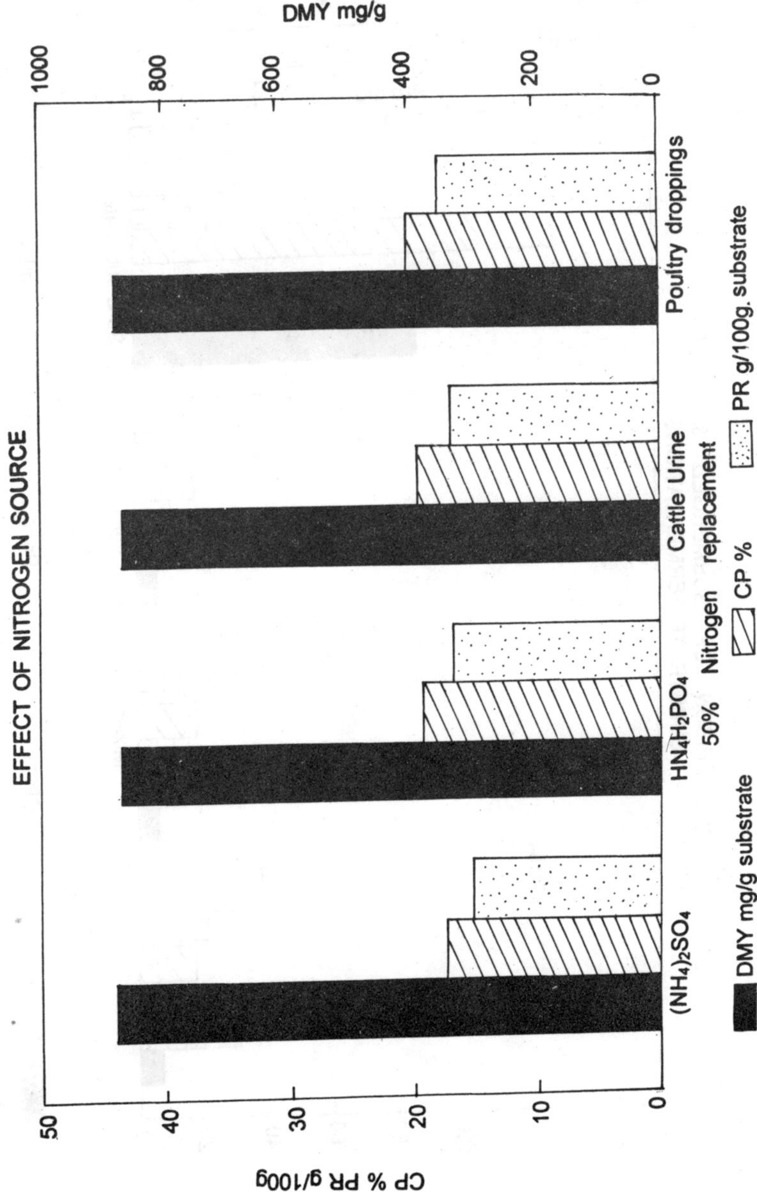
EFFECT OF NITROGEN SOURCE
DMY mg/g
0
200
400
600
800
1000
CP % PR g/100g
0
10
20
30
40
50
(NH4)2SO4
HN4H2PO4
Cattle Urine
Poultry droppings
50% Nitrogen replacement
DMY mg/g substrate
CP %
PR g/100g. substrate

Figure 5.6

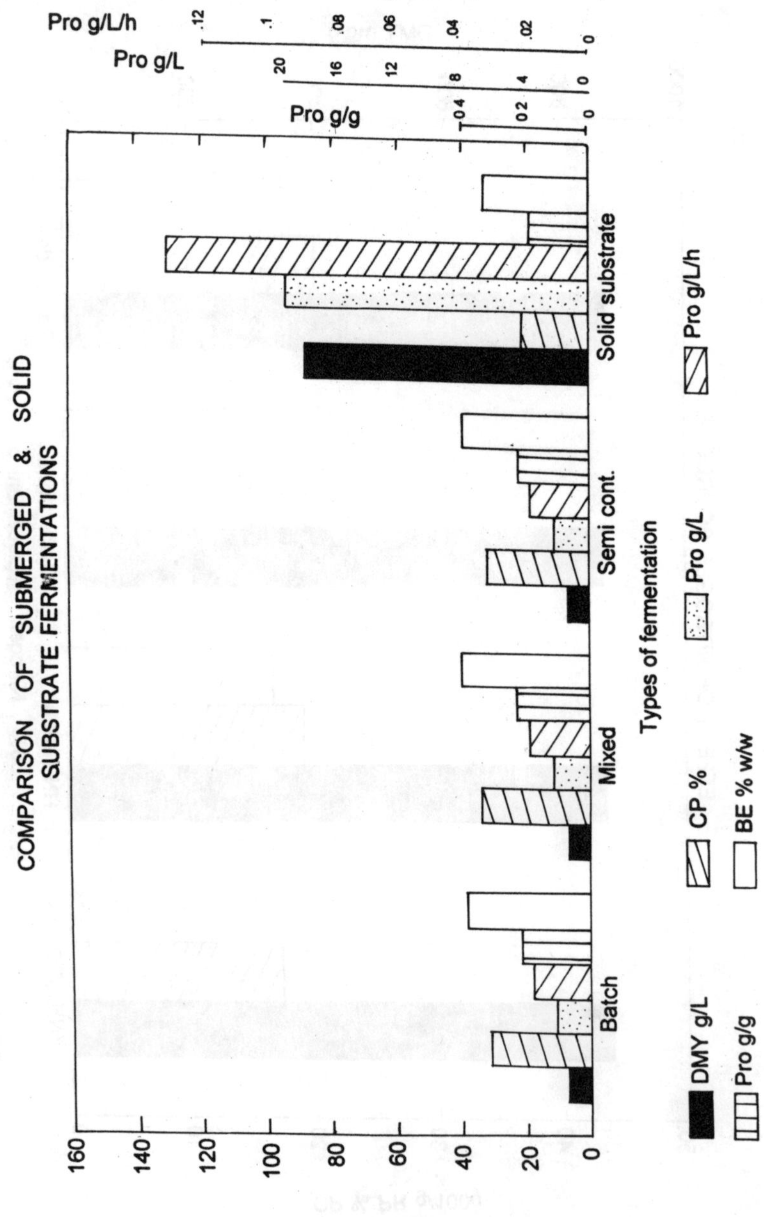
COMPARISON OF SUBMERGED & SOLID SUBSTRATE FERMENTATIONS
Pro g/L/h
Pro g/L
Pro g/g
DMY g/L CP % BE % w/w
Batch
Mixed
Semi cont.
Solid substrate
Types of fermentation
DMY g/L
Pro g/g
CP %
BE % w/w
Pro g/L
Pro g/L/h

Figure 5.7

Discussion

The basic advantage of the SSF in fully utilizing the absorptive properties of substrates like rumen ingesta was evident during the fermentation.

Milling and delignification of the substrate with alkali and heat treatment helped in improving the yield of proteins (Table 5.1). In SSF a solid material serves as a main source of nutrient for an organism which intimately associates with the surface and interstices of the material (Ralph, 1976). Hence an improvement in the yield may be explained by a change in the particle size - water - air relationship due to physical treatment or by the change in the porosity of the material with delignification (Zadrazil & Brunnert, 1982).

Han and Anderson (1975) reported sulphuric acid and heat treated straw to be a more efficient substrate than untreated straw. Chahal et al., (1981) found 4% w/w NaOH treated corn stover to be a superior substrate for SSF a compared to stover treated by other chemical methods.

Heat treatment of substrate prior to fermentation either at 121 C or at 70 C did show about 3g/100g improvement in the protein recoveries as compared to the nonsterile substrate (Table 5.2). However, the temperature of heating did not make much difference.

Sterilization or pasteurization prior to fermentation perhaps produces soluble organic substrates and also eliminates a part of competitive microflora which reduce the cellulose and hemicellulose content of the substrate. Ulmer et al., (1981) found that steam treatment as a method of sterilization did not significantly alter the protein production.

The optimum period of incubation for SSF was 6 days was a day more than that required for submerged fermentation. An incubation period longer than 6-7 days caused many irregularities in fermentation such as dehydration of the substrate, sporulation of the culture and a slight decrease in yield, due to perhaps, the lowering of pH.

Han et al., (1976a) reported an optimum period of 2-3 days. Pamment et al., (1978) found the growth rate of the organism to be 2-4 times slower in SSF than in slurry fermentation. Bajracharya and Mudgett (1979) and Ghai et al. (1980) reported a period of 4 days to be optimum for cutting down the incubation period from 10-12 days to 5 days, Chahal (1985) recommended pretreatment of substrate and also a correct C: N ratio. Ulmer et al. (1981) advised harvesting before the sixth day when sporulation and mycelial fragmentation begin.

Moisture seemed to play a crucial role in SSF of rumen ingesta as indicated by Table 5.4. 75% initial moisture content was most unsuitable of all the variables of moisture content. 60% moisture was evidently, the optimum since the yield was maximum 17.8g/100g substrate. However, a decrease in the moisture content to 45% seemed to partially affect the growth of the organism due to dehydration in the last phase of incubation.

Wang et al., (1979) and Kundu et al., (1983) considered moisture level to be a very important and vulnerable characteristic of SSF. Moisture levels less than 35% affect bacterial growth adversely, but a limitation of water levels sometimes affects the mobilization of microbes and nutrients.

Aidoo et al., (1982) stated that since the fermentation of moist solid substrate produces large quantities of heat, moisture levels and aeration affect the performance of the culture. In fact, the types of organisms to be used for SSF are limited to those which can grow at reduced moisture levels, namely fungi, yeasts and a few bacteria and streptomycetes. Hrubant (1975), Raiinbault et al., (1977) and Senez et al., (1990) found 40—45% moisture to be sufficient for SSF. However Prendergast et al., (1983) recommended a 70% moisture content.

The results obtained with additional aeration at 8 L/h (Table 5.5) indicate that aeration with water vapour saturated air influences the performance of the SSF favourably. Nearly 5-6% increase in the CP content of the biomass and a 4.4% improvement in protein recovery were recorded.

Since the thermal conductivity of lignocellulosic substrates is very low, (Aidoo et al., 1982), aeration is probably very important for exchange of metabolic heat, for making more oxygen available and also maintaining the relative humidity in the incubator.

Bajracharya and Mudget (1979) found air with a relative humidity of 70—80% to be very critical for SSF. Ulmer et al., (1981) concluded that the increase in protein content and cellulose degradation accompanying aeration were primarily due to ventilation of carbon dioxide rather than to an increased oxygen level in the fermentation flask.

The SSF of rumen ingesta with various N sources showed that a combination of ammonium sulphate and poultry droppings in a 50 : 50 ratio of N (w/v) is the most suitable for obtaining higher PR values.

Ammonium sulphate by itself at 3.5 gN/L is not an adequate source of N. The inclusion of KH_2PO_4 in ample quantities in the High Salt Solution makes the phosphate molecule of $NH_4H_2PO_4$ redundant for additional buffering activity unlike in submerged fermentation. Cattle urine did not prove to be as efficient as poultry droppings when combined with $(NH_4)_2SO_4$.

Han and Anderson (1975) found 4 N ammonia solution to be an efficient source of N while Kokke (1977) recorded the suitability of 5 *g* $NH_4H_2PO_4$ /100g of carob pods.

The results obtained in the present investigation agree with those of Moo Young et al. (1979b) who found animal manure to be a very good source of N, for obtaining higher yields of proteins.

An all optima SSF yielded a biomass with a CP of 21.4% and an overall protein recovery of 18.7g/100g with an increase of 19.8% of CP over the unfermented substrate.

These results are in agreement with those obtained by Chahal et al., (1981) who reported a 20-24% CP from 4% NaOH treated corn stover in 4-5 days and Veisturs et al., (1981) who reported production of 16-18% CP in steam treated straw with a mixed culture fermentation and 1214% CP in straw fermented with **Chaetomium celloulolyticum** alone after six days of incubation.

The results in this investigation are lower than those reported by Prendergast et al., (1983) who obtained a 32% CP on fermentation of NaOH treated wheat straw with **C. celluloyticum.**

Ghai et al. (1980) obtained a biomass with a 13.2% CP after 8 days of fermentation of alkali treated rice straw using **Myrothecium verrucaria.** Ulmer et al., (1983) produced a total of 15.5% CP from steam treated Feed lot waste fibres after fermentation with **C. cellulolyticum** for 7 days. Ulmer (1983) however reported one of the poorest yields of protein, 6-7% CP from alkali treated straw with a mixed culture of **Sporotrichum pulverulentum** and **Canadida utilis.** Neelkantan (1987) obtained 10% CP from wheat straw supplemented with 3000 ppm cattle urine N and 7.5% poutry excreta using **Neurospora sitophila.**

Thus it can be seen that the yields of protein from the SSF of rumen ingesta are comparable with and better than yields of SSF of many other lignocellulosics.

Comparison of Submerged and Solid Substrate Fermentation : (Table 5.8, Fig. 5.7). Submerged fermentation of rumen ingesta by any of the studied methods, with a rigorous control of pH, aeration and stirring yielded a total of 6-7 g/L of DMY since not more than 10g of the substrate could be taken in a fermentor of 1 litre working capacity.

Taking the yields of all the submerged fermentation methods as a whole the range of DMY was 6.68-6.98 g/L and its CP content ranged from 31.2 to 33.5% (Table 5.7). The protein recovery after 120 h of incubation was 2.14 to 2.22 g/L. Hence the protein productivity/L/h was. 0.0178-0.0186 g. Protein yield calculated on w/w basis was/ 0.214-0.224g/g substrate. The bioconversion efficiency (w/w) of the submerged fermentation assuming a 100% conversion of potential carbohydrate to fungal biomass per g of dry straw on a theoretical conversion factor of 0.565g/g was 37.9-39.3% (Patil, 1985).

In comparison, the SSF in a tray with an average of 100 g initial substrate/litre of medium, and 60% initial moisture content and aeration at 8 L/h, yielded 87.6 g of dry matter. Its CP content was 21.4%. The overall protein recovery was 18.7- g/L of medium in 144 h and the protein productivity was 0.1299 g/l/h. However, on a w/w basis the protein yielded of the substrate was .187 g/g and the bioconversion efficiency (w/w) of the SSF was 33.1%.

TABLE 5.8

Comparison of Submerged & Solid Substrate Fermentations

Type of Fermentation	*DMY g/L*	*CP %*	*Protein g/L*	*Protein g/L/h*	*Protein g/g subs-trate*	*Biocon-version efficiency % w/w*
Submerged						
Batch	6.85	31.2	2.14	0.0178	0.214	37.9
Mixed	6.68	33.5	2.24	0.0186	0.224	39.3
Semicontinuous	6.96	31.9	2.22	0.0185	0.222	39.3
Solid Substrate	87.60	21.4	18.7	0.1299	0.187	33.1

* assumes average value of 100g/L substrate during fermentation.

** percent conversion of potential carbohydrate to fungal biomass per g of dry straw based on a theoretical conversion of 0.565 g/g.

The SSF yielded a slightly less percentage of protein than submerged fermentation but there were many advantages, some of the more important being:

1. A large amount of rumen ingesta could be fermented per volume i.e., the space required for fermentation is much less as compared to submerged method.
2. The complexity of the equipment and the medium on a laboratory scale is much less.
3. Aeration is much easier and the process can be carried out under relatively non sterile conditions.
4. Product harvesting and drying costs are much lower than in submerged fermentation.

6

Nutritive & Toxicological Evaluation of the Mycoprotein

Chemical composition of fungal biomass is not a fixed entity and it depends greatly on the limiting substrate and environmental conditions (Mateles, 1979). The crude protein values (N x 6.25) include non-protein N such as nucleic acids. The amino acid values of a dietary protein should be comparable with a reference egg protein of FAO/ WHO (1965). Yeast, fungal and soya protein tend to be deficient in methionine contents for human and animal nutrition.

The acceptance of a novel protein supplement for animal feeds necessitates extensive testing, not only of its chemical and nutritional characteristics but also of its safety and efficiency *in vivio* (Norris & Richmond, 1981).

The live weight gain, feed intake and feed efficiency ratios of various sources of SCP have been compared with traditional sources of proteins in various experimental animals like broiler chicken (Vogt. 1973; Rys et al., 1975; D'Mello, 1978), white leg horn chicks (Lee & Yang, 1981), layers (Pethukova et al., 1982), young pigs (pearson et al., 1978 and Steven & Zimmerman, 1979), lambs (Nath et al., 1979), goats (Singhal & Mudgal, 1983) and ruminants (Vijjan et al., 1978 and Gupta, 1988).

Microbial proteins may contain considerable amounts of nucleic acids, unmetabolized ingredients and secondary metabolites with toxic properties. To ensure the safety of the product in animals, the body weights, organ weights, haematological and clinical chemistry and histopathological changes in some organs are studied by feeding trials (Spingarn & Weisburger, 1979).

Fungal and yeast proteins have been toxicologically evaluated in various hosts like chick embryos, (Neumamova et al., 1986), chicken (Farstad, 1977), rats (Pronczuk et., 1971), mice (Dey, 1977), albino rats (Moo Young et al., 1978 and Ek & Erikson, 1978), buffaloes (Desai, 1986) and bullocks (Sampath, 1987).

Materials and Methods

Amino Acid Analysis: A sample of the product by SSF containing 10 mg of protein (N x 6.25) was hydrolysed with 1 ml of 6 N HC1 at 110 ± 1C for 24 h in evacuated tubes. After hydrolysis the acid was evaporated under reduced pressure in a rotary evaporator. The residue was dissolved in 0.2M Sodium citrate buffer, pH 3.2. Amino acid analysis of the sample and a standard was performed with a buffer sequence of pH 3.2, 4.5 and 6.45 in a "LKV Biochrome 4151 Alphaplus" amino acid analyser.

Feeding Trial in Poultry

Experimental design and plan of work: The feeding trial was conducted on eighteen 2 day old Rhodowhite chicks obtained from Central Poultry Breeding farm, Aarey, Bombay. These birds were divided into 3 groups of 6 each and housed in separate cages after weighing.

Feed Mashes: Deoiled rice bran (DROB) a conventional source of N in poultry mash was replaced completely (5% of total feed by (A) Untreated, dried, milled rumen ingesta, and (B) Fermented biomass, dried and milled. A feed mash (C) with 5% DROB was taken as control.

The high crude fibre content and other differences in the composition of rumen ingesta and groundnut extract, did not permit the replacement of groundnut extract, a conventional feed protein (ISI, 1968). The percent chemical composition of the different feed mashes and the supplements was determined on a dry matter basis.

The different poultry mashes A, B and control mash C (Table 6.2) which were isonitrogenous and isocaloric were allotted randomly to the three different groups of chicks. Rovimix, a vitamin supplement was added to the mash at 0.18g/kg and Fucox = a coccidistat was administered at 0.5g/litre of drinking water, in the first week.

Housing and Management: The 3 groups of birds were housed in three disinfected cages with wire netting bottoms. Adequate warmth, water level and cleanliness were maintained.

Feeding Schedule: Group feeding was practised and weighed quantity of the feed was supplied **ad lib** to the birds. The left over material was weighed on the next day at 8.30 a.m. so as to calculate the daily feed consumption. The average daily and weekly feed consumed per bird, for each group, were calculated.

Live Weights: The body weighs of individual chicks were recorded at weekly intervals. The average weekly live weights and gain in weight per chick were calculated for each group. The weekwise and overall feed efficiency was calculated for each group.

Haematological studies: All the birds were bled at the end of eight weeks, from the right jugular vein. 5 ml of blood was collected in sodium oxalate solution. Using Neubaeur's haematometer and Hayem's fluid, total RBC counts were made.

Hemoglobin was estimated using Sahli's method. Packed Cell Volume (PCV) was determined in Wintrobe tubes. Differential WBC counts were made from fresh bloodsmears by Giemsa's method.

Carcass evaluation: After the eight week experimental period the birds were starved for 12h and sacrifised. Carcass evaluation was performed by the method of Panda (1971).

The dressed weights were determined after complete bleeding and removal of feathers. Edible carcass yield of individual birds was recorded after removal of head, digestive tract and legs. Heart, liver, gizzard (empty), kidney and spleen were weighed individually and the average weight of the organs for the 3 respective groups was calculated. The percentages of dressed weight and weight of the different organs were calculated and compared with live weights.

Post mortem Examination and Histopathological Analysis: All the slaughtered birds were examined for any gross abnormalities in the organs like liver, spleen and kidney, due to toxicity. The samples of each of the above organs were collected in 10% formalin and were examined histologically after due processing at the Department of Pathology, Bombay Veterinary College, Bombay.

Results

Amino Acid Analysis: The results of the amino acid analysis of the biomass protein, along with the FAO reference protein are given in Table 6.1 and Fig. 6.1.

Almost all the essential and non essential amino acids were present in the Mycoprotein. Except for lysine, methionine and tyrosine, the biomass protein was richer in all other aminoacids as compared to the FAO reference protein.

Comparision of Feed Mashes: The formulae of the poultry mashes A,B, C are given in Table 6.2 and the proximate analysis of the feed mashes in Table 6.3. The protein content of all the 3 mashes ranged from 22.8% to 24.7%; the other extract content ranged from 1.4% to 1.8%; the crude fibre ranged from 4.2% to 5.8%, and the Nitrogen free extract was 60.1% to 61.8% in all the 3 mashes.

The average weekly feed consumed per bird (Table 6.4) for group A was 189.56 g, for group B 183.61 g and for control group C it was 198.67 g indicating that the control group C consumed maximum feed, while the group B consumed minimum feed.

TABLE 6.1

Essential Amino Acid Pattern of Biomass Protein g/100g Protein

Amino acid	*Biomass Protein*	*FAO reference egg protein*
Lysine	2.7	4.2
Threonine	6.2	2.8
Valine	5.2	4.2
Methionine	1.4	2.2
Isoleucine	6.2	4.2
Leucine	5.8	4.8
Tyrosine	2.2	2.8
Phenylalanine	3.2	2.8

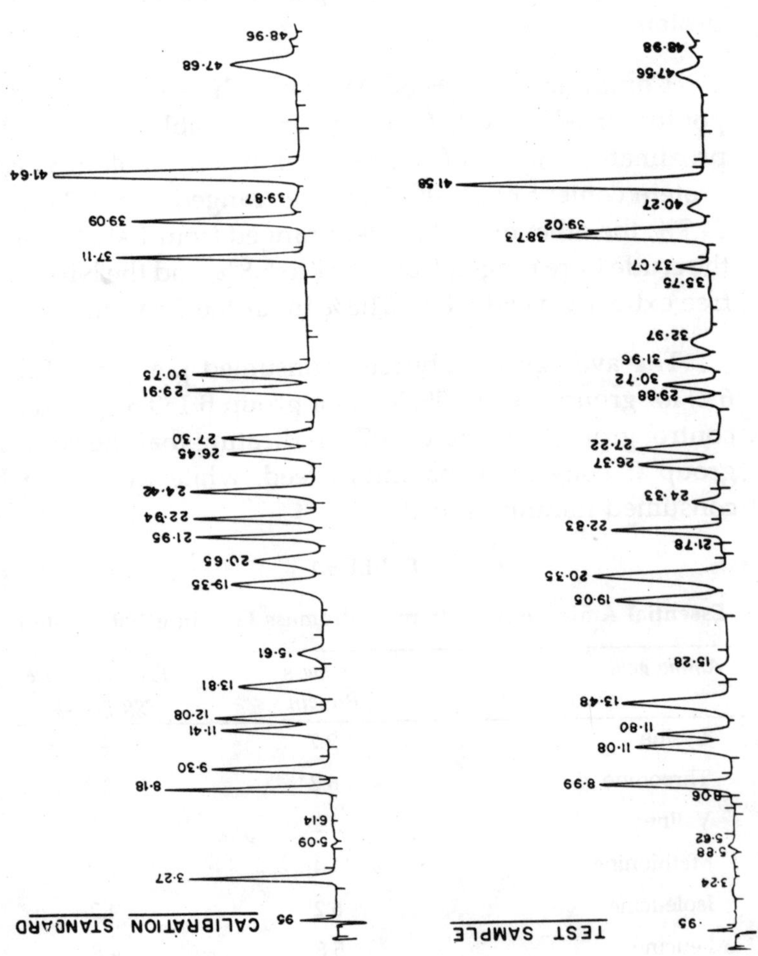
CALIBRATION STANDARD
95
3·27
5·09
6·14
8·18
9·30
11·41
12·08
13·81
15·61
19·35
20·65
21·95
22·94
24·42
26·45
27·30
29·91
30·75
37·11
39·09
39·87
41·64
47·68
48·96
TEST SAMPLE
·95
3·24
5·88
5·62
8·06
8·99
11·08
11·80
13·48
15·28
19·05
20·35
21·78
22·83
24·33
26·37
27·22
29·88
30·72
31·96
32·97
35·75
37·07
38·73
39·02
40·27
41·58
47·56
48·98

Figure 6.1

TABLE 6.2

Feed Ingredients In Different Feed Mashes

Ingredients	*Mashes*		
	A	*B*	*C*
Maize	55.0	55.0	55.0
Ground Nut extract	28.5	28.5	28.5
Fishmeal	10.0	10.0	10.0
Mineral mixture	1.5	1.5	1.5
Deoiled rice bran	-	-	5.0
Ovendried rumen ingesta	5.0	-	-
Ovendried biomass protein	-	5.0	-
Total	100	100	100

Rovimix (Vitamins A + B_2 + D_3 + K) @ 0. 1 g/kg

TABLE 6.3

Proximate Analysis of Feed Mashes and Supplements

Nutrients	*Feed Mashes*			*Dried rumen*	*Protein*
	A	*B*	*C*	*ingesta*	*biomass*
Dry matter	89.52	90.56	92.34	88.56	90.01
Crude Protein	22.85	24.06	24.69	7.69	29.86
Ether extract	1.65	1.77	1.47	1.59	2.01
Crude fibre	5.72	4.35	4.15	38.38	25.37
Total ash	9.68	8.05	7.87	9.98	8.65
Nitrogen free extract	60.10	61.77	61.82	42.42	34.11

Average Weekly Live Weights and Gain In Weights: Table 6.5 indicates that the weekly live weighs of the birds were normal in all 3 cases. However, compared to the control group C, the Group A (rumen ingesta) showed a lower average weight through out the trial. Group B (biomass protein) showed comparable live weights to the control Group C. (Table 6.5).

TABLE 6.4

Average Weekly Feed Consumed (g) per Bird and Feed Efficiency of The Birds

Weeks	**Feed Consumed (g)** *Group*			*Weeks*	**Feed Efficiency** *Group*		
	A	*B*	*C*		*A*	*B*	*C*
I	56.08	51.66	51.50	I	1.79	1.56	1.53
II	100.08	112.83	112.16	II	1.83	1.76	1.78
III	151.67	160.50	165.00	III	1.99	1.84	1.85
IV	222.06	221.66	229.16	IV	2.49	2.28	2.31
V	226.21	246.67	239.99	V	2.61	2.41	2.44
VI	242.81	255.83	259.17	VI	2.93	2.63	2.77
VII	246.76	261.03	265.69	VII	3.24	3.04	2.98
VIII	270.83	260.66	266.67	VIII	3.58	3.27	3.23
Average/ week/bird	189.56	196.36	198.67	Average	2.56	2.35	2.36
Average/ bird/day	27.08	28.05	28.38				

The gain in weights too was normal in all 3 cases, but Group A was slow in gaining weight as compared to Groups B and C. Average gain in weight per bird per week was 71.57 g for Group A, 80.85g for Group B and 81.09g for group C.

The Average Weekly Feed Efficiency: (Table 6.4) For Group A this was 2.56, group B 2.35 and Group C 2.36 indicating a better feed efficiency of groups B and C as compared to Group A. Group B showed a feed efficiency which was comparable to Group C.

TABLE 6.5

Average Weekly Live Weight (g) and Gain in Weight (g)

Weeks	*Live Weight*			*Gain in Weight*		
	A	*B*	*C*	*A*	*B*	*C*
2 days	35.00	36.16	35.66	-	-	-
I	66.33	69.33	69.33	31.33	33.17	33.67
II	122.33	133.50	132.33	55.0	64.17	63.00
III	198.50	220.66	221.67	76.17	87.16	89.34
IV	287.66	317.33	320.67	89.16	97.33	99.01
V	374.33	419.66	419.00	86.67	102.33	98.33
VI	456.50	517.00	512.50	82.87	97.34	93.50
VII	532.66	602.67	601.66	76.16	85.67	89.16
VIII	608.33	682.33	684.33	75.67	79.66	82.67
Total	-	-	-	572.52	646.33	648.68
Average	-	-	-	71.57	80.85	81.09

Haematological Studies (Table 6.6): The hemoglobin was in the range 10.3 to 14.8g/100 ml blood, which is in the normal range. The PCV was 21.8% for Group A, 23.5% for the Group B and 24% for Group C, all of which are in the normal range.

The RBC counts per cu.mm were 2.28×10^6 for group A, 2.75×10^6 for group C indicating the closeness of values of Group B & C. The differnetial WBC count indicated no abnormality in the blood of any of the 3 groups.

Carcass Evaluation of the Birds: (Table 6.7) after 8 weeks indicated that the percentage of dressed weight of all 3 groups was 91.92% of average live w· ight.

The weight of edible carcass of all the three groups was between 70-73%, which is normal. The weight of all the organs was in the normal range.

TABLE 6.6

Haematological Observations On 8 Week old Birds

	Groups		
	A	*B*	*C*
Hemoglobin (g/1 00 ml)	10.3	12.6	14.8
PCV (%)	21.8	23.5	24.0
RBC/cu.mm(x 10^6)	2.28	2.75	2.79
Differential WBC count %			
Neutrophils	23	22	21
Eosinophils	2.5	2	2
Basophils	2	2.5	2
Monocytes	6.5	5.5	7
Large lymphocytes	17	21	26
Small lymphocytes	49	47	42

Histopathological Examination

General: All organs except 2 livers of Group *A* appeared grossly normal. These 2 livers showed fatty metamorphosis. No tumours were encountered. Histologically, all the organs except those described below were normal.

Liver: Livers of 2 birds of Group A showed fatty metamorphosis which could be graded as mild to moderate. The portal sheath showed fatty infiltration, lymphocytic aggregation and round cell hyperplasia. There were no inclusion bodies.

Kidney: The microsections of kidney of 2 birds of all groups, i.e., A, B, and C displayed some tubules which showed cloudy swelling and granular degeneration. Some tubules also showed desquamation of the epithelial cells. The glomerulae were however, normal.

Spleen: Spleen of one bird of Group A showed lymphoid hyperplasia.

TABLE 6.7

Carcass Evaluation (g) After 8 Weeks

	Groups		
	A	*B*	C
Average Live weight	608.75	687.50	656.25
Average dressed weight	560.00	632.75	602.50
% " -"	91.92	91.75	91.80
Av. wt. of Edible carcass	430.00	491.25	478.75
% . -"-	70.49	71.45	72.80
Av. Wt. of Liver	14.98	17.05	17.50
% -"-	2.62	2.47	2.66
Av. Wt. of heart	3.28	3.45	3.45
% -"-	0.54	0.51	0.55
Av. Wt. of Kidney	5.88	6.63	6.25
% -"-	0.96	0.97	0.95
Av. Wt. of spleen	5.1	5.4	5.8
% -"-	1.28	1.35	1.45
Av. Wt. of gizzard	17.78	15.42	16.68
%-"-	2.8	2.24	2.41

Discussion

Though the fermented biomass is intended primarily for supplementation of large animal diet, the pilot feeding trial was conducted in poultry since they are the fastest and more efficient feed converters among laboratory animals.

The amino acid content of the biomass protein was comparable to that of the FAO reference protein. Deficiency in methionine, lysine and tyrosine have been observed for fungi by a number of authors Peitersen, 1975b; Solomons, 1985).

The deficiency in lysine and other amino acids may be also explained by the fact that this biomass was cultivated on nutrient media without supplementing with any protein source, unlike those used by many authors (Peitersen, 1975 b).

Gain in body weight is a very sensitive parameter for monitoring the nutritive value and toxic effects of a test substance in animals. The lack of any significant difference in the feed consumption, the live weights and gain in body weights of the three groups, indicated normal acceptance of the test diets.

However, the feed efficiency of Group A was poor, compared to the other two groups. The feed efficiency of the biomass protein feed group B was similar to that of the control group C, indicating a good nutritive value of the biomass protein.

There was no alteration in any of the haemotological parameters proving absence of any acute toxicity. No significant differences were detected in the edible carcass weights or organ weights of the 3 groups.

In the histological examination, the test Group A showed pronounced changes in the liver, kidney or spleen tissue. Fatty changes in the liver indicated slight toxicity. However, the pathological changes in the kidneys of all the 3 groups indicated that a substance other than biomass protein/ rumen ingesta may have been responsible for these histological changes.

Shacklady et al. (1969) found a 10% hydrocarbon yeast diet to be nutritive as well as non toxic in pigs and poultry. Liver and renal damages were however reported in chicks and mice fed on yeast SCP as well as other high protein diet by Farstad et al. (1977), Tuse' et al., (1981) and Sinha and Arora (1987).

Vijjan et al., (1978), Stevan and Zimmerman (1979) and Desai (1986) determined yeast SCP to be an excellent protein feed stuff in large animals.

Feeding of mice with **Trichoderma viride** sp. (Peitersen, 1975b), **Chaetomium cellulolyticum** (Moo Young et al., 1978) **Trichosporon** SCP (Schoch & Schlatter, 1983); **Penicillium janthinellum** (Srinivasan et al., 1983) did not provoke any acute toxic or pathological reactions.

The Paecilo protein (Romantschuk, 1975) and **Fusarium graminearum** CMI 145425 (Anderson & Solomons, 1983) have been granted clearance for animal feeding and human consumption respectively.

Summarising the results, it can be concluded that Mycoprotein from rumen ingesta had a good nutritive value in poultry. However, it cannot be concluded whether some of the histological changes observed were due to rumen ingesta/Mycoprotein or simply due to a high protein diet.

7

Summary and Conclusions

This study was undertaken in order to utilize rumen ingesta—a slaughter house waste-for recycling into feed proteins.

The rumen ingesta was made up of 36% cellulose, 27% hemicellulose and 13% lignin. A pretreatment with 5% NaOH and heat made fermentation of the substrate more productive.

On enrichment and isolation, 90 cellulolytic isolates were obtained. After primary and secondary screening for its suitability as a protein organism, a mold isolate was selected. Its identity was established as **Penicillium simplicissimum.** A Cellulolytic bacterial isolate was also selected for mixed culture inoculum and tentatively identified as a **Cellulomonas sp.**

Various parameters of submerged fermentation were standardized in shake flasks. 1% substrate concentration in **Trichoderma viride** medium without peptone, a 5% mycelial inoculum, initial pH 5-5.51 Incubation for 5 days with continuous shaking and 350 mg N/L of ammonium dihydrogen phosphate were found to be optimum for protein production.

Scale up processes in a pilot fermentor, by batch fermentation with and without pH control, by mixed culture fermentation and by a semicontinuous fermentation were standardized to obtain a yield of 33.5% crude protein, compared to 28.5% CP in shake flasks. The incubation period was shortened to 4 days by mixed culture fermentation or semicontinuous fermentation.

An innovative solid substrate fermentation of rumen ingesta, in trays placed in humidified incubators was designed and standardized. 5% NaOH pretreatment, preheating at 70 C for 30 min for pasteurisation of substrate, 3.5 g of N/L in the form of ammonium sulphate and poultry dropping extract, 60% initial moisture content, aeration at the rate of 8 L/h and incubation) time of 5 days were found to be optimum. The biomass has a CP content of 21.4%.

The protein productivity by submerged fermentation was 0.0178 - 0.0186 g/L/h while that of SSF was 0.1299 g/L/h. However, on w/ w basis, the protein yield was 0.214 - 0.224 g/g and 0.187 g/g for submerged and SS fermentations respectively and the corresponding biconversion efficiencies were 37.9-39.3 % and 33.1%.

Though the w/w yield of protein was lower than in submerged fermentation, the SSF has many advantages related to the process controls, initial substrate concentration and harvesting, which makes it a more attractive and useful method for rural and industrial use.

The eight week feeding trial of the final biomass protein at 5% levels in poultry indicated a good nutritive value and a general absence of any acute toxicity. However, in view of some of the preliminary findings, further studies of nutritive and toxicity evaluation are warranted.

Although wastes like rumen ingesta are unaesthetic and unattractive as substrates for recycling into proteins, the problem of their disposal is too urgent and too enormous for us to be complacent or indifferent. Viewed dispassionately, on the basis of its chemical composition and the different methods available to ferment it, bioconversion of rumen ingesta will provide a lasting solution to the problems of pollution of our environment and the protein malnutrition in our animals.

References

Ahmed, A.U. (1982), "Study of Fungi from Soils in Maharashtra with Special Reference to Cellulolytic Fungi." Ph.D. thesis, Poona University.

Aidoo, K.E.; Hendry R.; Wood, B.J.B. (1982) *Adv. in Appl. Microbiol.* **28**: 201-237.

Akin, D. E.; Benner, R. (1988). *Appl. and Environ. Microbiol.* **54**: 1117-1125.

Alien, A.L.; Andreotti, R.E. (1982). *Biotech. Bioeng. Symp.* **12**: 451.

Alien, A.L.; Mortensen, R.E. (1981). Biotech. *Bioeng.* **23**: 2641.

Ali, R.; Zaidi, Z.H. (1984). *Pak. J. Science and Indus. Res.* **27(1)**: 47-50.

Anderson, C; Solomons, G. L. (1983): eds. In "The Applied Mycology of **Fusarium",** Cambridge Univ. Press, 231-250.

Andren, R.E.; Ericksson, R.J.; Mediros, J.E. (1976). "Enz. Conv. Cellulosic Materials". Tech. and Appli., eds. Gaden, E.L.; Mandels, M.H.; Reese, E.T.; Spano, L.A. Inter Sc. Publ.: 177.

Andreotti, R.E.; Mandles, M.; Roche, C. (1978). *Proc. Bioconversion Symp.* (1977). T.K. Ghose, IIT, Delhi: 249-267.

A.O.A.C. (1970). *Official Methods of Analysis.* AOAC., Washington, 11th Edn.: 1-20.

Araujo, A. (1978). "Studies on Cellulases from Marine

Fungi Using Agricultural Wastes." M. Sc. thesis, Bombay University.

Araujo, A. (1984). "Hyper-production of Cellulase by **Aspergillus terreus.** ATCC 52430 isolated from Coastal Waters in India". Ph. D thesis, Bombay University.

Araujo, A.; D' Souza, J. (1980). J. Ferment. Technol. **58** (4): 399-401.

Armstrong, D.W.; Martin, S.M. (1983) Biotech. Bioeng. **25**: 2567.

Atal, C.K.; Thakur, R.N.; Sastry, K.S.M.; Pandotra. S.B.; Bhatia, A.K, (1978). Indus. Ferm. Symp. Jammu, March 4-6.

Bagga, P.S.; Sandhu, D.K. (1987). J. Ferment. Technol. **65**: 635-642.

Bagool, R.G. (1982). "Studies on Cellulolytic Fungi of Maharastra State". Ph. D thesis, University of Pune.

Bailey, M.; Enari, T.M.; Linko, M. (1975). eds. Symp. on Enzyrmatic Hydrolysis of Cellulose". Aulanko, Finland.

Bailey, J.E.; Ollis, D.F. (1977). Biochem. Engineering Funda. McGraw-Hill, Inc. N.Y.; 163.

Bajpai, P.; Bajpai, P.K. (1988) Enzyme Microbiol. Technol. **10**:280 283.

Bajracharya, R.; Mudgett, R.E. (1979). Biotech. Bioeng. **21** (4): 551-560.

Baldensperger, J.; Lemur, J.; Hannibal, L.; Quinto, P.J. (1985) Biotech. Letters. 7 (10): 743-748.

Bastawde, K.B.; Deshpande, V.V.; Joglekar, A.V.; Lakshmi kantham B.C.; Mishra, C.; Phansalkar, S.B.; Mala Rao; Seeta, R.; Srinivasan, M.C.; Jaganathan, V. (1978). "Bioconversion of Cellulosic Subs. into Energy, Chem. and Microbial Protein Ghose. T. K. Ed. N. Delhi., 143-151.

Bergey's Manual of Determinative Bacteriology (1974). Buchnanan R.E.; Gibbons, N.E., eds. 8th Edn. William's & Wilkins Baltimore.

Betrabet, S.M.; Dasani, U.P.; Bhatt, I.G.; (1968) Text. Res. J. **38:** 1189.

Bhattacharya, A.K. (1974) "Cellulolytic Organising", M. Sc. Thesis Bomba Univ.

Bhattacharya, A.N.; Taylor, J. C. (1975) J. Anim. Sci. **41,** 1438.

Bisaria. V.S.; Ghose, T.K. (1981) Enz. Microbiol. Technolo. 3: 90.

Blum, R.; Stahl, W.H. (1952) Text. Res J. **22**: 178.

Brown, D.E.; Halsted, D.J.; Howard, P. (1975) in "Symp. on Enz. Hydrolisis of Cellulose" eds. Bailey, M.; Enari, T.M.; Linko, M. Aulonko, Finland.

Bucholz, J.P.; Godelmann, B; Dietrichs, H.H. (1981) Process Biochem. **16** (1): 37.

Bungay, H.R. (1983). in "Production & Feeding of SCP", Proc of a COST workshop. "Ferranti, M.P.; Fiechter, A eds. Appl. Sc. Zurich. 15-22.

Cabrera, D.S.; Mayorga, H.; Espiosa, R.; Rolz, C. (1974) Proc. IV. Int. Cong. Fd. Sc. and Tech. 4: 296-301.

Callihan, C.D.; Clemmer, J. E. (1979). Economic Microbiology. **4** ed. Rose, A. H., Aca. Press, London: 71-286.

Carrizales, V.; Saenz, D. (1984) Proc. 7th Int. Biotech. Symp., New Delhi, Feb. 19-25: 470.

Chahal, D.S. (1982). Adv. In. Agri. Microbiol. Ed. Subbarao, N. S., 551-583.

Chahal, D.S. (1984). Biotech. Bioeng. Symp. **14**: 425-433.

Chahal, D.S. (1985). App. And Env.Microb. **49** (1): 205-210.

Chahal, D.S.; Graw W.D (1971) Ind. Phyto.Path. **21** : 80

Chahal, D.S.; Cheema, S.P.S. (1971) Plant Science. **3** : 86

Chahal, D.S., Ishaque, M. (1984). Proc. of 7th Int. Biotech. Symp.-II, New Delhi, Feb. 19-25,: 458

Chahal, D.S.; Singh, A.; Dhillon, G. S.; Kalra, M. S. (1978) "Indus. Ferm. Symp." Jammu, India, March 4-6.

Chahal, D.S.; Moo-Young, M.; Vlach, D. (1981) Biotech. Bioeng. **23**:2417-2420.

Chahal, D.S.; Swan. J.E. Moo-Young, M. (1977). Dev. Ind. Microbiol. **18**:433-442.

Chang, M.M.; Chou, T.Y.C.; Tsao, G. T. (1981) Adv. Biochem Eng. **20**: 15.

Chang, P.; Pond, W. G.; Kingsbury, J. M.; Walker, E. F. (Jr); Krook, L. (1978). J. Anim. Sci. 47 (2): 319-330.

Chang. W.T.; Hsly, W.H.; Lai, M.N.; Chang P.P. (1980) Ferment. Technol. **54**: 450-458.

Chidambereswaran, P.K.; Balasubramanya, R.H.; Bhatawadekar, S.P. Sreenivasan, S.; Sundaram, V. (1986) Enzyme Microb. Technol **9**: 561-567.

Christias, C.; Couvaraki, C.; Georgopulos, S.G.; Macris, B.; Vomvoyanni, V. (1975). Appl. Microbiol. **29**: 250-254.

Christiensen, H.R. (1910). Cent. Bakt. Parasitenk (II) **27**: 449.

Considine, P.J.; Hackett, T.J.; Coughlan, M. P. (1987) Biotechnol. Lett. 9: 131-134.

Cowling, E.B. (1975). Biotech. Bioengg. Symp. **5**: 163-182.

Cowling, E.B.; Kirk, T. K. (1975) Biotech. Bioeng. Symp 5: 163.

Daugalis, A.J.; Bone, D.H. (1978). Biotech. Bioengg. **20**: 1639-1640.

Dave, R.V. (1983). "Biodegradation of Cellulose." M. Sc. thesis, Bombay University.

Dehority, B.A.; Johnson, R. R. (1961). J. Dairy Science, **44**: 2422-2249.

Deonar Abattoir (2001) Report for internal circulation. (Unpublished data).

Desai, H. (1986) "Feeding trials of SCP... in buffaloes". Ph.D. Thesis. Gujarat Agri. Univ. Anand, Gujarat.

Detroy, R.W.; Lindenfelser, L.A.; St. Julian, G. (Jr); Orton, W.L. (1979). *Biotech. Bioeng. Symp.* **10**: 125.

Dey, B.P. (1977). Dissertation Abst. Int. **38** (2): 573 (c. f. *Nut Abstr. Rev.* **49B** (8): 3190 (1979)).

Dhillon, G.S.; Kalra, K.L.; Ghai, S.K.; Kahlon, K.L.; Kalra, M. (1980). In "Recycling of Agricultural and Industrial Waste' Proc, Symp. Ludhiana, Kalra,, M. S. Ed. & Pub,: 77-85.

Dhillon, G.S.; Singh, A.; Kalra, M. S. (1982) J. Food Sc. & Tech. **19**: 74-78.

Difco Manual (1969).

Difco Manual of Dehydrated Culture Media and Reagents for Microbiological & Clinical Lab. Proc., Difco Labs. Detroit, U. S., 245.

D'Mello, F.J.P. (1978). *J. Sc. Food Agric.* **29**: 453-460.

D'Souza, J. (1972). "Studies on Fungi Isolated from the Marin Environment" M. Sc. thesis, Bombay University. Dubos, R..J Dubos, R.J (1928) J Bact. **15**; 223.

Dubos, R.J. (1928). J. Bact. **15**; 223.

Dudhbhate, J.A. (1985). Studies on the the Microbial Degradatioi of Pulp and Paper Mill Waste." Ph. D. Thesis, Pune University.

Durand-Chastel, H.; Clemment, P. (1975) in "Proc. of 9th. Int. Cong of Nutrition" (Karger, Basel, Switz.) **3**: 85-90.

Ek. M.; Eriksson, K. E. (1975) Biotech. Bioeng. **17**: 327-348.

Ek. M.; Eriksson, K. E.; (1978) in "Biconversion of Cellulosic Substances into Energy, Chemicals and Microbial Protein". Symp. Proc., Ghose, T. K., Kd. II T, New Delhi.: 449.

El-Nawawy (1969) In "Global Impact of Applied Microbilogy-3". Freitas, Y. M.; Fernandes, F. (1971). eds., 421-428.

Emert, G.H. (1974): Adv. Chem Ser. 136 Am. Chem. Soc.: 79-100

Eriksson, K.E. (1974). Norsk Skogsindustri **5**: 125.

Fan, L.T.; Gharpuray, M. M.; Lee, Y. H. (1981). In Biomass, Energy Production and Conservation" 2nd Symp., Vol. II: 29.

Fan, L.T.; Lee, Y. H.; Gharpuray, M. M. (1982). Adv. Biochem. Eng. 23: 167-176.

FAO/WHO (1965). Expert Committe on Protien Requirement Report, S. No. 37, F. A. O., Rome.

F.A.O. Production Year Book (1999).

Farstad, L. (1977). Acta. Agric. Scandinavia **27**: 129&137.

Feldman, K.A.; Lovett J. S.; Tsao, G. T. (1988). **Enzyme Microb. Technol. 10**: 262-272.

Ferranti, M.P; Fiechter, A (1983). eds. "Production & Feeding of **SCP", Proc of a COST workshop.** Appl. Sc. Zurich.

Fink, H.; Schlei, I.; Ruge, U. (1953). Physiol. Chem. **292**: 251-263.

Freitas, Y.M.; Fernandes, F. (1971). eds. "Global Impact of Appl. Microbiology-3" (969), Dec. 7-12, Bombay University.

Galas, E.; Pye, R.; Romanowska, I. (1987). Proc. of 4th Euro. Cong. on Biotechnol. ed. Neijssel et al. **2**: 27.

Gallo, B.J.; Andreotti, R.; Roche, C.; Ry, D.; Mandels, M. (1978). Biotech. Bioeng. Symp. **8**: 89.

Garg, S.K.; Neelkantan, S. (1981). J. of Fd. Sc. and Tech. **18**: 64.

Garg, S.K.; Neelkantan, S. (1982a) Biotech. Bioeng. **24**: 109&125.

Garg, S.K., Neelkantan, S. (1982b) Biotech. Bioeng. **24**:2407-2417.

Gaur, A.C.; Neelkantan, S.; Dargan, K. S. (1984) Organic Manures Tech. Bull., ICAR, New Delhi.

Gellender, R.M. (1981) Chem, Int. **1**: 21-25. (c. f. Solomons, 1985).

Ghai, S.K; Singh, A; Dhillon, G.S; Kahlon, S.S; Kalra K.L; Kalra M.S. (1980). "Recycling of Agricultural and Industrial Waste", Proc. Symp. Ludhiana, Pub. & ed. Kalra, M. S: 87-94.

Ghate, N.P. (1984). "Studies on the Mycoflora of Industrial Waste from Paper and Pulp Factories in Maharashtra, ", Ph. D. Thesis Poona University.

Ghose, T.K. (1978). Ed. "Byconversion of Cellulosic Substance into Energy, Chemicals and Microbial Protein", Symp. Proc II T., New Delhi.

Ghose, T.K.; Ghosh, P. (1978). App. Chem Biotechnolo. **28**: 309 329.

Ghose, T.K.; Kostic (1969). Symp. Adv. Chem. Ser. (ACS): **95** 415 (c. f. Ferranti & Fiechter, 1883, 10).

Ghose, T.K.; Sahai, V. (1979). Biotechnol. Bioeng. **21**: 283.

Gilkes, N.R.; Langford, M.L.; Kilburn, D.G.; Miller, R. Warren, R.A. (1984). J. Biol. Chem. **259**: 10455.

Gong, C.S.; Tsao, G.T. (1979). Ann. Rep. Ferment. Proc. 3: 111-140.

Gonsalez, V.S.A.; Moo-Young, M. (1981). Biotechnol. Lett **3**: 148.

Gould, J.M. (1985). Biotech. Bioeng. **27**: 225.

Grethlein, H.E. (1978). Biotech. Bioeng. **20**: 503-506.

Griffin, H.L.; Kaneshiro, T.; Nelson, B. F.; Slonker, J. H. (1975) In "Symp. on Enzymatic Hydrolysis of Cellulose". Bailey M Enari, T. M.; Linko, M. eds. Aulanko. Finland, 419-432.

Gritzali, M.; Brown, R. D. (1979). Adv. Chem. Ser. **181**; 237.

Grohmann, K.; Torget, R.; Himmel, M. (1985). Biotech. Bioeng Symp. **15**. 59-80.

Gupta, B.N. (1988). Report, "Bioconversion of Crop Residue India, -Nutritional Aspects", NDRI, ICAR, Karnal.

Gupta, D.P.; Heale, J. B. (1971). Biotech. and Bioeng. **19**; 1331 1349.

Hajny, G.J.; Reese, E. T. (1969). Adv. Chem. Series **95**: 7.

Halliwel, G. (1957). J. Gen. Microbiol. **17**: 153.

Han, Y.W. (1978. Adv Appl. Microb. **23**: 199-153.

Han, Y.W.; Anderson, A. W. (1975) Appl. Microbiol **30**, 930-934.

Han, Y.W.; Callihan, C. D. (1974). Appl. Microbiol. **27**: 159-165.

Han, Y.W.; cheeke, P. R.; Anderson, A. W.; Lekpayoon, C. (1976a) Applied Environ. Microbiol. **32**: 799&802.

Han, Y.W.; Dunlop, C. E.; Callihan, C. D. (1971) Food Technol **25**: 130-154.

Han, Y.W.; Grant, G. A.; Anderson, A. W.; Lu, P. L. (1976b). Feedstuff. April: 17-20 (c. f. Aidoo et al., 1982).

Han, Y.W.; Srinivasan, V. R. (1968) Appl. Microbiol. 1140-1145.

Han, Y.W.; Lillehoj, E.; Timpa, J.; Ciegler, A. (1980) Biotech. Letters **2**: 397.

Harwood, J.H.; Pirt, S.J. (1972). J. Appl. Bact. 35: 597.

Hendy, N.A.; Wilke, C.R.; Blanch, S. (1982). Biotech. Letters, **4:** 785.

Hendy, N.A.; Wilke, G.R.; Blanch, S. (1984). Enzyme. Microb. Technol. **6:** 73.

Hesseltine, C.W. (1977). Process Biochem. **12.** 24-27 & **12:** 30-32.

Hesseltine, C.W. (1965). Fungal Biotechnology, eds. Smith. J.E.; Berry, D.R.; Kristensen, B. **4,** 1-24.

Howell J.A; Stuck, J. (1975) Biotech, Bioeng **17,** 873-893.

Hrubant, G.R. (1975). Appl. Microbiol. **30:** 13-119.

Humphery, A.E.; Moreira, A.; Armiger, W.; Zabriskie, D. (1977). Biotech. Bioeng. Symp. 7: 45-64.

Hungate, R. E. (1944). J. Bact. **48:** 499-513.

Hutton, J.B.; Jurry K.E.; Gunn, KC. (1965) NZ. J. Agric. Res: 8, 479.

Icchhaponani, J.S.; Lodhi, G. N. (1976). Indian j. Anim. Sc. **45** (45): 234.

Imsenecki, A.A. (1968). In "Ecology of Soil Bacteria" eds. Gray T. R. G. Parkinson, D., Univ. Toronoto Press: 257-269.

I.S.I. (1968) ISI specifications for broiler feeds: ISI, 1374.

Ivarson, K.C.; Morita, H. (1982). Appl. Environ. Microbiol. **43:** 643-647.

Jagganathan, V.; Rao, M.; Deshpande, V.V.; Mishra, C.; Lakshmikantha, B.C.; Bastawde, K.B.; Kulkarni, V.H.; Phansalkar, S.B.; Joglekar, A.V.; Srinivasan, M.C. (1975). Paper Pres, at Int. Sym. on Enzym. Eng. Poona.

Janus, J.M. (1978). In "Byconversion of Cellulosic Substance into Energy, Chemicals and Microbial Protein", Symp. Proc., Ghose, T. K. Ed, II T, New Delhi. 469-478."

Jobling, A. (1986). Developments in Food Proteins, ed. Hudson, B.J.F., Elsevier Applied Sc., 37-56.

Joglekar, R.; Clerman, R.J., Ouellette, R.P.; Cheremisinoff, P.N. (1983) "Biotechnology in Indiustry". Ann Arbor Sc. Butterworth Group: 49.

Kalra, M.S. (1980). ed. "Recycling of Agricultural and Industrial Waste", Proc. Symp. Ludhiana, Pub. Kalra, M. S.

Kamakura, M.; Kaetsu, I. (1982) Biotech. Bioeng. **24,** 991-997.

Kamakura, M.; Kaetsu, I. (1983). Proc. Biochem. 18 (5): 14.

Kamakura, M.; Kaetsu, I. (1984). Agric. Wastes **9**: 279-287.

Kamikubo, T.; Tanaka, M.; Taniguchi, M.; Morita, T. (1981). Adv. in. Biotech. 2: 311.

Kamra, D.N.; Zadrazil, F. (1985). Biotech Letters, 7:.335-340.

Kelkar, P.V. (1977). "Fungi in Maharashtra", Ph. D. thesis, Pune University: 203-217.

Kellerman, K.F. Mcbeth I..G. (1912). Centra. Bakt. Prasitenk II 34:485.

Khandeparker, V.G. (1976). Cellulases from **Penicillium funiculosum** (**F4**) Ph. D. thesis, Bombay University.

Kim, J.E.; Lebault, J.M. (1981). Eur. J. Appl. Microbiol. Biotechnol **13:** 151.

Kirk, T.K.; Farrell, R.L. (1987). Ann. Rev. Microbiol. **41:** 465-505.

Klappach, G.; Weichert, D.; Meyer, D. (1984). in "Proc.-7th Int. Biotech. Symp-2, New Delhi: 461.

Klein, D.A.; Rockhill, R.C.; Eldridge, J.P.; Park, J.E. (1970) Tappi, **53**: 1469-1472.

Knapp, J.S.; Howell, J. A. (1980). In "Topics in Enzyme & Ferm. Biotechnol., ed. A. Wiseman, Ellis Horwood, N. Y.: 85-128.

Koenigs, J.W. (1972). Phytopathology **62**: 100.

Kokke, R. (1977). J. Appl. Bact. **43**: 303-307.

Kristensen, T.P. (1978). Eur. J. Appl. Microbiol. **5:** 155-163.

Kundu, A.B.; Ghosh, B.S.; Ghosh, B. L.; Ghose, S.N. (1983). J. Ferm. Technol. **61**: 185-188.

Ladisch, M.R.; Lin, K.W.; Volch; M; (1983) Enzyme Microb Tech. 5 82-98. Apsite, A. F.; viesturs, U. E. (1984) Biotech. Bioeng. **26:** 1465-1474.

Laukevics, J.J.; Aspite At... (... 1465-1474)

Lee. P.K.; Yang, U.F (1981). J. Taiwan Livestock Res. **14:** 21-37. (c. f. Nutr. Abst. Rev. (1983), **53B**, 1087).

Lillehoj, E.B.; Han, Y.W. (1983). Biotech. Bioeng. **25**: 2077-2084.

Linko M. (1977) Adv. Biochem. Eng. **5:** 27.

Lilly, V.G.; Barnet, C. (1951). Physiology of Fungi. Mcgraw Hill, N. Y. Linko, M. (1977). Adv. Biochem. Eng. **5:** 27.

Litchfield, J.H. (1979). Bicrob. Technol. **1:** 93. eds. Peppier, H. J.; Perlman, D. Acad. Press.

Litchfield J.H. (1985) Comprehen. Biotech. 3: 463.

Litchfield, J.H., Overback, R. C.; Devision, R. S. (1963). J. Agri. Food, Chem. **11:** 158-162.

Macris, B.J.; Kokke, R. (1978) Biotech. Bioeng. **20:** 1027-1035.

MacDonald, D.G.; Mathews, J. F. (1979). Biotech. Bioeng. Symp. **21:**1091.

Mandels, M.; Hontz, L.; Nystrom, J. (1974). Biotech. Bioeng. **16:** 1471-1493.

Mandels, M.; Stenberg, D. J.; Andreotti, R. (1975). In "Symp. on Enzymatic Hydrolysis of Cellulose". Bailey, M.; Enari, T. M.; Linko, M. (1975). eds. Aulanko, Finland. 81.

Mandels, M.; Reese, E. T. (1957). J. Bact. **73**:. 269-278.

Mandels, M.; Reese, E. T. (1964). Develop. Ind. Microbiol. **5**: 5.

Mandels, M.; Weber, J. (1969). Amer. Chem, Soc. **95: 447.**

Mandokhot, U. (1987). Personal communication from Jt. Commissioner, Ministry of Agri., N. Delhi.

Manning, K. (1981). J. Biochem. Biophy, Methods, **5. (4)**: 189-202.

Mark, H. (1954) in "High Polymers", eds Ott. E; Spurlin, H. M.; Graffm, M. W., Inter Sc.: **5:** 217.

Meteles, R.I. (1979). The Physicology of SCP Production: Current State, Furure Prospects (SGM Symp. 29) eds, Bull, A. T.; Ellwood, M.; Ratledge, C. Cambridge Univ. Press, London.

McGill, A.E.J.; Annette, D.; Jackson, N. (1978). Record Agri. Res. **26:** 93-95 (c. f. Nutr. Abstr. Rev. **49B** (8), 3251).

Miller, G.L. (1959). Anal. Chem. **31:** 426.

Miller, T.F.; Srinivasan, V. R. (1979). Paper Presented ACS Divn., Microbiol. & Biochem. Technol. Meet. Washington, Sept. 9 14.

Miller, T.F.; Srinivasan, V. R. (1983). Biotech. Bioeng. **25:** 130.

Mitra, G.; Wilke, C. R. (1975). Biotech. Bioeng. **17:** 1-3.

Molina, U.E.; Perotti, N. I.; Frigerio, C. I.; Cordob, P. R. (1984); App. Microbiol. Biotech. **20:** 135-139.

Montenecourt, B.S.; Eveleigh, D. E. (1977). Appl. & Environ. Micrbiol. **33:** 178-183.

Moo-Young. M.; Chahal, D.S.; Stickney, B. (1981). Biotech. Bioeng. 23: 2407-2415.

Moo-Young, M., Chahal, D.S.; Swain, J.E.; Robinson, C. W (1977). Biotech, Bioeng. **19:** 527-538.

Moo-Young, M., Chahal, D.S.; Vlach, D. (1978). In "Bioconversion of Cellulosic Substance into Energy, Chem & Microbial Protein" Symp. Proc., II T, "Ghose, T. K. Ed., New Delhi: 457.

Moo-Young, M., Chahal, D.S.; Vlach, D. (1979a). Biotech. Bioeng. **20** 107-118.

Moo-young, M., Daugulis, A.J., Chahal, D.S.; MacDonald, D.G. (1979b). Process Biochem. **14 (10):** 38-40.

Mukatak, S.; Tada, S; Takahashi, J. (1983). J. Perm. Technol. **61:** 615.

Mukhopadhyay, S.N. (1980). Adv. In Biotech. 3: 277-280.

Mukhopadhyay, S.N.; Pathak, A.N. (1973). Chem. Age. India, **24 :** 583-587 (c. f. Aidoo et at., 1982).

Muralidhar Rao, N. (1987) Adv. in Meat Research, eds. Khot, J.B.; Sherikar, A. T.; Jayarao, B. B.; Pillai, S. R. Red & Blue Cross, Bombay: 142-150.

Murase, G.; Kendrick, B. (1986). Biotech. Lett. **8** (1): 25-30.

Murray, W.D. (1986). Appl. and Env. Microbiol. 51:710-714.

Nagy. G., Milagros, V.K.B.; Aniko, S.O. (1975) Biotech. Bioeng. **17:** 1823-1826.

Nath, K.; Vijjan, V.K.; Krishna, G.; Ranjhan, S.K. (1979). Indian J Anim. Sc. **43** (3): 199-202.

Neelakantan, S. (1987). In "Biol., Chem. & Phy. Treatment of fibrous crop residues as animal feed. "Indo-Dutch Project ICAR, New Delhi. Singh, K.; Flegel, T. W.; Schiere, J. B. eds.: 37-45.

Neijssel, O.M., Meer, R.R.V.; Luyben, K. Ch. A.M. (1987). "Proc. 4th Eur. Cong. Biotechnol. June 14-19. Elsevier, Amesterdam.

Neumamova, V., Fassationa, O. Vesela, D.; Vesely, D. (1986). "Veterinarni Medicina **31** (11): 687.

Nisizawa, K. J. (1973). Ferment Technol. **51**. 267-304.

Norris, J.R.; Richmond, M.H. (1981). Essays in Microbiology, John Wiley, chichester,: 6 / 30.

Nystrom, J.M.; Diluca, P.H. (1978) "Biconversion of

Cellulosic Substance into Energy, chem. & Microbial Protein", Symp. Proc., II.T, Ghose, T. K. Ed., New Delhi., 293-304.

Omeliansky, V. (1902). Centr. Bakt. Parasitenk-II 8: 289.

Opoku, A.R.; Adoga, P. A. (1980). "Enzyme Microbiol. Technol **2** (3): 241-243.

Oshima, M. (1965). Wood Chemistry Process Eng. Aspects. Noyes. Dev. Corp. N. Y. (c. f. Rehm & Reed, 1983).

Pamment, N., Robinson, C., Hitton, J.; Moo Young, M. (1978) **20**: 1735-1744.

Paquot, M.; Herman, L. (1983). In "Production & Feeding of SCP"., Proce of a COST workshop". Ferranti, M. P; Fiechter, A. eds., Zurich: 118-119.

Prardez-Lopes; Gonsalez, Y. (1973). J. Ferm. Tech. **51** (8): 619.

Patil, R.V. (1985), "Studies on Cellulases", Ph. D. thesis, Pune Univ.

Panda, B. (1971). Ind. Poultry Gaz. **55**: 21.

Pearson, V.; Ewan, R. C.; Zimmerman, D. K. (1978). J. Anim. Sc **47**: 488-491.

Peitersen, N. (1975a). Biotech. Bioeng. **17**: 361-374.

Peitersen, N. (1975b). Biotech. Bioeng. **17**: 1291-1300.

Peitersen, N. (1975c). In "Symp. on Enzymatic Hydrolysis of Cellulose". "Bailey, M.; Enari, T. M.; Linko, M. eds, Aulanko, Finland: 407-431.

Peitersen, N. (1977). Biotech, Bioeng, **19**: 337-348.

Petterson, L.G.; Axio, F. U. B.; Berghem, L. E. R. (1972). Proc. I. F. S. Symp. **4** "Fermentation Technol. Today': 727-729.

Pethukova, E.A.; Ryazanov, G.P.; Kazhdan, V.E.; Dubinskaya, A.V.; Strezhneva, T.V. (1982). Refrantivnyi Zhurnal, **58**: 459 (c.f. Nutr. abstr. 53B) 9, 3307.

Prendergast, P.; Booth, A.; Colleran, E. (1983). In "Production & Feeding of SCP", Proc of a COST workshop. "Ferranti, M. Fiechter, A. (1983). eds. Appl. Sc. Zurich.: 96-100.

Pritchard, G.I., Pigden, W.J.; Minson, D. J. (1962). Can J. Anim. Sc. **42:** 215.

Pronczuk, A., Bernacka, T.; Bartnik, J. (1971). Boczniki Technologi Chemii Zywrnosci **20:** 63-75, (c. f. Nutr. Abstr. Rev. **42** (1): 683, 1972).

Quinn, J.P.; Marchant, R. (1979). Eur. J. Appl. Microbiol. Technol. 6: 897-904, (c. f. Tanaka and Matsuno (1985).

Rai, S.N.; Mudgal, V.D. (1987). Ind. J. Anim. Nutr. **4** (1): 5-11.

Raimbault, M.; Deschamps, F.; Meyer, F; Senez, J. C., (1977). Int. Conf. GIAM V, Bangkok.

Ralph, B.J. (1976): Food Technol. Aust. **28**, 247-251. (c. f. Aidoo, et al. 1982).

Ramachandran, L. (1982). Food Planning-Some vital Aspects, Allied Publ., New Delhi: 102-103.

Ramachandra, M., Craford, D.L.; Pomento, A. L. Ill (1987). Appl. Environ. Microbiol. **53:** 2754-2760.

Ranjhan, S.K. (1980), Paper pr. at Proc. RRAI, PAU, Ludhiana, ed. & Pub. Kalra, M. S. (1980): 7-17.

Rao, M.N.A., Mithal, B.M., Thakur, R.N, ; Sastry, K.S.M. (1983) Boitech, Bioeng, **25**: 869-872.

Rao, R.R., Deshmukh, S. S.; Srinivasan, M. C. (1984). Biotech. Lett. 6 (7): 461-464.

Rao, V.V. (1978) "Degradation of Bagasse by Microorganisms" M Sc. Thesis, Bombay University.

Rautella, G.S.; Cowling, E.B. (1966). Applied Microbiol. **14:** 889 892.

Reddington, S.; Brown, D.E. (1987). In "New Process of Waste Water Treatment & Recovery", ed. Mattock. G. Publ. Ellis Horwood: 349-378.

Reddy, C.A.; Erdman, M. D. (1977). "Biotech, Bioeng. Symp. **7**: 11-22.

Reddy, G.V.K. (1986). "Improved utilization of paddy straw by applying ensiling techniques using animal excreta". Ph. D. thesis, Andhra Pradesh Agri. University.

Reese, E.T. (1962) ed. "Advances in Enzymic Hydrolysis of Cellulose and Related Materials. "The Amer. Chem. Soc., Pergamon Press, Oxford.

Rehm, H.J.; Reed. G. (1983). ed: Biotechnology **3**, Verlag Chemie.

Reid, I.D. (1979) Can. J. Bot. **57**: 2050-2058.

Report C.F.G. (1987) Committee on Fodder and Grasses National Waste Dev. Board, New Delhi: **26**.

Report NCA (1980) of National Council of Agril. For NABARD., New Delhi: 18-19.

Rhodes, R.A.; Orton, W. L. (1975). Trans Am. Soc. Agric. Eng. **18**: 728-733 (c. f. Aidoo et at (1982)).

Ridgeway, J.A. (Jr.); Lappin, T. A.; Benjamin, B. M.; Coirns, J. B; Akin, C (1975). Food Eng. **49** (6): 95 (c. f. Litchfield, 1985).

Ringpfeil, P., Beck, D.; Hadeball, W.; Kreuter, T.; Heinritz, H.J. (1980). In 6th Inter, Conf. GIAM. Lagos, Academic Press. 233-244.

Roberts, R.S., Sondhi, D.K.; Bery, M.K.; Colcord, A.R.O.'Neil, D. J. (1980). Biotech. Bioeng. Symp. **10**: 125.

Rockewll, P.J. (1976). "SCP from Cellulose and Hydrocarbon." Noyes Data Corpn. N. Y.

Romantschuk, H. (1975). In "Single Cell Protein"-II eds. Tannenbaum, S.R. and Wang, D.I. C., M.I.T. 355-356.

Romantschuk, H.; Lehtomaki, M (1978) Process Biochem. **13** (3), 16-29.

Rose, R.H. (1979). ed. Microbial Biomass-Economic Microbiology Vol. **4** Academic Press, N. Y.

Rosen, W.; K. Schuegerl (1983). In " Production & Feeding of SCP", Proc of a COST workship. "Ferranti, M. P; Fiechter, A. eds. Appl. Sc. Zurich., (1983). 87-89.

Rys. R; Koreleski, J.; Kuchta, M. and Skotnicki, J. (1975). Acta Agralia 15 (2): 81-94 (c. f. Nutr. Abstr. Rev. 47B (11); 3295, 1977).

Ryu, D.; Andreotti, R.; Mondles, M.; Gallo, B.; Reese, E. T. (1979). Biotech Bioeng, **21**: 1887-1903.

Sacco, M.; Millet, J.; Aubert, J.P. (1984). Ann. Microbiol. A**135**: 485.

Saddler, J.N.; Meshartnee, M, ; Yu, E.K.C.; Brownell, H.H. (1983). Biotech, Bioeng. Symp. **13** 225-238.

Sahai, V.; Ghose, T. K. (1978). In "Byconversion of Cellulosic Substance into Energy, Chemicals and Microbial Protein", Symp. Proc., II T Ghose, T. K. Ed., New Delhi.: 269.

Sampath S.R. (1987) In "Biol., Chem. & Phy. treatment of fibrous crop residues as animal feed. "Singh, K.; Flegal, T. W., & Schiere, J. B. (1987) eds. "Indo-Dutch Project, ICAR, 225-228.

Sandhya, S.; Joshi, S.R.; Swaminathan, T. (1984). J. Sc. & Ind. Res. **43:** 452-458.

Sanyal, A.; Kundu, R. K.; Sinha, S. N.; Dube, D.K. (1988) Enzyme Microb. Technol. 10: 85-90.

Sarkar, J.; Prabhu, K.A. (1982). J. Ferment. Technol. **60:** 297-303.

Schoch, U.; Schlatter, C (1983). In "Production & Feeding of SCP", Proc. of a COST workshop. Ferranti, M.P.; Fiechter, A. eds. Appl. Sc. Zurich., 173.

Schurz, J. (1978). In "Bioconversion of Cellulosic Substance into Energy, Chemicals and Microbial Protein", Symp. Proc., "Ghose, T. K. Ed. II T, New Delhi.": 37.

Scrimshaw, N.S. (1968). "Single Cell protein", eds. R. I. Mateles S. R. Tannenbaum, MIt, Cambridge: 3-7.

Tetrault, P.A. (1930). Centr. Bakt. Parasitenk/II, **81**: 38.

Thakur R.N.; Rao, M.N.A.; Mithal, B.M.; Sastry, K.S.M. (1982), Indian J. Miarob. **22(2)**: 160.

Thomke, S.; Rundergren, M.: Eriksson, S. (1980). Biotech. Bioeng. **22**: 2285-2303.

Toyoma, H.; Yokoyama, T. Shinmyo, A.; Okada, H. (1984). J Biotechol. **1**, 25.

Toyoma, N. (1976) Biotech. Bioeng. Symp. **6**: 207-219.

Trivedi, S.M.; Ray, R.M. (1985) Fermentation Tech. **63(3)**: 299-304.

Tuse, D; Russel, L.A.; Hseigh, D.P.H. (1981). Adv. in Biotech. **2**:363.

Ulmer, D.C. (1983). In "Production & Feeding of SCP.", Proc.of a COST workshop. Ferranti, M.P.; Fiechter, A. eds. 76-79.

Unmer, D.C.; Leisola, M.S.A.; Schmidt. B.H.; Fiechter, A. (1983) Appl. Environ, Microbiol. 45: 1795-1801.

Ulmer, D.C.; Tengrady, R. P.; Murphy, V. G. (1981). Biotech. Bioeng. Symp. 11:449-461.

Updegraff, D.M. (1971). Biotech. Bioeng. Symp. **13**: 71.

Viesturs, U.E.; Apsite, A. F.; Laukvics, J.J.; Ose, V.P.; Beker's M.J. (1981). Biotech. Bioeng. Symp. 11: 359.

Vijjan, V.K.; Krishna, G.; Nath K.; Ranjhan, S. K. (1978) Ind.J. Anim. Sci. **48** (9): 665-668.

Vogt, H. (1973). Archiv fur Geflugelkunde **37(6)**: 346-237 (c. f. Nutr Abstr. Rev. 44 (12): 8357, 1974).

Vogt, K.Z; Staffeldt, E. E. (1977). Dev. Ind. Microbiol. **18**: 571.

Vrati, S.; Verna, J. (1983), Ferment, Technol. **61**: 157-162.

Waksman, S.A.; Skinner, C. E. (1926). J. **12**: **57-84.**

Walseth. C.G. (1952), Tappi **35**: 233-238.

Wang. D.I.C., Cooney, C.L.; Demain, C.L.; Humphrey, A.E.; Lilly, M. d. (1979). Ferm & Enz. Technol. John Wiley, N. Y.: 218.

Wayman, M.; Lord, J.H.: Hinomea, R. (1880) ACS Symp. series **90** 183-210.

Wayman, M.; Parekh, R.S.; Parekh, S.R. (1987). Biotechol. Lett. **9**: 435.

Whittle, D.J.; Kilburn, D.G.; Warren, R.A.J.; Miller, R.C. (Jr.) (1982) Gene, **17**: 139.

Winkler, M. (1983). Topics in Enzyme and fermentation Biotech. ed. Alan Wiseman, **7**: 217-306.

Wood, T.M. (1975) Biotech. Bioeng. Symp. **5**: 111-137.

Wyllei, T.D. And Morehouse, L.G. (1978). Ed. Mycotoxic fungi, Mycotoxins and Mycotoxicoses, Hand book 2, Acad, Press, N. Y.

Wyman, C.E.; Spindler, D.D. Grohmann, K.; Lastick, S.M. (1988). Biotech. Bioeng. Symp. **17**: 221-238.

Yamanke, Y; Wile, C.R. (1976). Sym. AICHE National Meet. April, 1976.

Zadrazil, F. (1983). In "Production and Feeding of SCP", Proc. of a COST workshop. Ferranti, M. P.; Fiechter, A. eds.: 76-79.

Zadrazil, F.; Brunnert, H. (1982) *Eur. J. Appl. Micro. Biotech.* **16**: 45-51.

Index

□□□